Grav

THE LEGEND OF RAY GRAVELL

To Mari, Manon and Gwenan

Grav

THE LEGEND OF RAY GRAVELL

Stories from friends and family

RHYS MEIRION (ED.)

First impression: 2021

© Copyright Rhys Meirion, the contributors and Y Lolfa Cyf., 2021

The contents of this book are subject to copyright, and may
not be reproduced by any means, mechanical or electronic,
without the prior, written consent of the publishers.

Thanks to the following for the photographs:
BBC, Media Wales, Phil Bennett, Huw Llywelyn Davies,
Mari Gravell, Carolyn Hitt, Dafydd Hywel, Roy Noble and Emyr Wyn.

Cover image: *South Wales Evening Post*
Cover design: Y Lolfa

ISBN: 978-1-912631-18-6

Published and printed in Wales
on paper from well-maintained forests by
Y Lolfa Cyf., Talybont, Ceredigion SY24 5HE
website www.ylolfa.com
e-mail ylolfa@ylolfa.com
tel 01970 832 304
fax 832 782

Cofio Graf
Remembering Grav

Grav oedd Grav, dyna'i gryfder, 'Odw i'n iawn?'
Grav was Grav, that was his strength, 'Am I right?'
    Dyna oedd ei bryder;
    That was his worry;
  Ond daw swn, medd Duw o'i sêr,
  But there comes a noise, says God from his stars
Grav o hyd, Grav a'i hyder.
Always Grav, Grav and his confidence.

Aneirin Karadog

Contents

Foreword: Rhys Meirion   9

Fellow School Pupil
Adrian Howells   13

Rugby Players
Clive Rowlands   18
Gerald Davies   21
Gareth Edwards   26
Phil Bennett   30
Simon Easterby   38
Ollie Campbell   40
Bill Beaumont   43
Delme Thomas   46
John O'Driscoll   50

Family and Close Friends
Mari Gravell   52
Gwenan Gravell   63
Manon Gravell   64
Nanette Jones   69
Sarra Elgan   70
Elin Hefin   71
Janet Rowlands   74

Mansel Thomas   77
Eamon Duffy   80

Commentators
Huw Llywelyn Davies   88
Gareth Charles   94
Nic Parry   97
Eleri Siôn   99
Dot Davies   101

Producers
Geraint Rowlands   102
Keith Davies   107
Sion Thomas   123
Marc Griffiths   127
Dewi Wyn Williams   128

Actors and Correspondents
Gary Slaymaker   130
Dafydd Hywel   133
Emyr Wyn   137
Rhys Bleddyn   141
Gareth Roberts   142
Frank Hennessy   145
Roy Noble   150
Carolyn Hitt   154
Sulwyn Thomas   156
Geraint Lloyd   161
Mal Pope   162
Aneirin Karadog   163

Foreword

Rhys Meirion

Without question, one of Wales' greatest ever characters now and for ever more was the enigma from Mynydd-y-Garreg, Ray Gravell. He was a man that touched the lives of all who had the privilege of meeting him, with his innocent excitement and genuine interest making everyone in his presence feel special.

Even though we lost Ray over ten years ago, I have noticed how he is still a topic of conversation when I meet and chat with people over the length and breadth of Wales. And as we chat about him, without fail, everyone has a 'Grav tale' or two. Some that make us laugh out loud, some that make us admire the man even more than we already did, and also some that bring a lump to the throat.

I had the privilege of meeting Ray only about half a dozen times. The first time was at the National Eisteddfod in 2001. I was at the BBC offices and Ray saw me. He finished the conversation he was having with someone else and made a beeline towards me, and as he approached me, shouting 'Rhys Meirion, Rhys Meirion,' he reached out to shake my hand. He did so with such exuberance I feared my arm might come free from its socket!

'Waw, you have a hell of a voice!' he said. Then, turning to the people around us he shouted, 'What a voice, what a voice, tip top, tip top bois bach!' while still shaking my hand vigorously! And then came the sentence that I will never forget: 'I would give up my Wales and Lions caps to have a voice like yours.' If he only knew how much of a hero he was to me, my having followed rugby since I was a child. I felt ten foot tall! He made me feel very special, and I shall never forget that feeling.

I later remember going to Mold Rugby Club where Ray was speaking at a dinner as part of Robin McBryde's testimonial year with the Scarlets. The club was packed; Ray was at his best and had everyone in the palm of his hand. Ray could seamlessly bridge between humour, sincerity and profoundness as a speaker; people would be laughing with hilarity one minute, and then you could hear a pin drop the next as he would share an emotional or inspiring anecdote. At the end of one story I saw him looking over at me, and off he went.

'I see that Rhys Meirion is here. What a voice! He's got a beautiful tenor voice, he's young, good looking with a mop of dark hair, he's handsome [by this time I was consumed with embarrassment on the one hand, and bursting with pride on the other amidst such praise and compliments] and when he sings those high notes men cry and women get so excited... BASTARD!'

Well, the room erupted, everyone was beside themselves laughing. Ray was waving at me apologising with a mischievous smile on his face.

Yes, there are a myriad of 'Grav tales' out there, some of them known to most of us because they get told repeatedly by public speakers or are written in autobiographies and so on. But, after being in the company of a number of Grav's friends and former colleagues recently, it became apparent to me that there were hundreds of 'Grav tales'. Some are, of course, hilarious, but so many remind us of his valour, his genuineness, his kindness, and that he was such an inspiring character. It would be such a shame for these tales and anecdotes to be lost for ever, and that's my inspiration in trying to collect as many 'Grav tales' as I can and record them in a book, ensuring that they will be available for everyone to enjoy for years to come.

He was unique; there will never be another Ray Gravell.

Fellow School Pupil

Adrian Howells

I have such sweet memories of our days as former fellow pupils of Carmarthen Grammar School for Boys, between 1963 and 1969, to share with you.

I started in 1963 and Ray followed a year later after passing his 13+, as it was then, from Burry Port Secondary Modern. And I have to admit, from day one, he was like a hurricane! He wasn't an academic child but he was full of enthusiasm for rugby, for the Welsh language and for Owain Glyndŵr, his hero!

Now then, there was a very important process to be followed on the first day, and that was to find out which house you were going to belong to. It was going to be either Arthur (blue), Glyndŵr (red), Myrddin (white) or Llywelyn (black). It all depended on the first letter of your surname. I was in Arthur, and I believe that's where Ray should have been, but following a short meeting with the teacher that was in charge of classifying, Ray was able to secure his place in the house of Glyndŵr. But not only just being in the house of Glyndŵr, he was also made captain as well! And, of course, all the rugby and athletic trophies in our year for the next five years went to Glyndŵr. We didn't have a chance when Owain Glyndŵr himself was facing us on the fields of play!

I don't have to mention that Ray was a rugby player and athlete who was ahead of his time, even in those early days. He represented Carmarthenshire Under-16s a year early, and captained them a year later.

My biggest claim to fame in my rugby career is that I played in the same team, for a whole year, with Ray Gravell and Roy Bergiers in the first team of Carmarthen Grammar School for Boys, 1968–69. Ray was at scrum half in those days, Roy was in the centre, and I was on the wing when I was in the sixth form. It was a very successful year, with the Gram beating everybody: Llanelli Grammar School, Neath, Gowerton, Whitland, as well as Llandovery College. At the end of the season we went on a tour to The Wirral to play two games, beating Wallasey Grammar School before our final game of the season against Birkenhead Park School. The headteacher of Birkenhead Park at that time was John Gwilliam, the captain of the Grand Slam winning Wales team of 1950 and 1952, who also played for Wales the last time we beat the All Blacks back in 1953. John Gwilliam played for Wales a total of 23 times and was captain for 11 of them.

Well, this was the most important game of our lives – it was more or less an international match between the best school team in Wales and the best independent school team in England, in front of the biggest crowd we had ever played in front of. I remember getting onto the bus, and the team having a lecture from the captain Phil Thomas and the teacher Elwyn Roberts about the importance of the game, but it was Ray who was the inspiration.

'This is an international boys, this is England against Wales. They are not thinking about whether they are going to beat us, but by how much they are going to win,' was just one of his passionate outbursts. He insisted that we all sang 'Calon Lân' as loud as we could in the dressing room before going onto the pitch. Birkenhead responded in good spirit with a song of their own, but I won't declare what Ray had to say about that!

I won't say much about the game, just to say that we lost 0–25, and that the captain of Birkenhead Park, John Howard, scored all the points. As you can imagine, Ray wasn't very happy. But after we all congratulated the opposition and admitted that they were the better team on the day, Ray had a completely unexpected invitation. John Gwilliam, the Birkenhead headteacher, asked if Ray would be willing to sit next to him at the dinner. Former captain of Wales, a member of the victorious Welsh team against the All Blacks, and one of the legends of Welsh rugby, asking for the company of a young lad to discuss the game. Incredible.

Another memory. In 1967, just before the O Level exams, Ray, myself and another five pupils created history by becoming the first ever pupils of the 5X class. It was a class created to get us to learn a bit of maths. But I can tell you now, the experiment was a total failure. The teacher faced with this task was Mr Llewellyn from Gowerton. He had played as a centre for Neath in the '50s and had played against Lewis Jones. We discovered this thanks to Ray, after he asked a question in the middle of a lesson, 'Did you ever play against Lewis Jones, sir?' And that's how things carried on; every lesson would start with a conversation about rugby, before Mr Llewellyn had had enough one day and gave us a long lecture about the importance of education. 'You'll get no success in life by concentrating only on rugby!' I can hear him saying it now. And then, following the lecture, we all had to stand in our turn to say what our ambition was in life. One said to be a fireman. I wanted to be a reporter, and there were a few farmers. When it was Ray's turn it was quite simple, 'To play rugby for Wales, sir.' And the rest is history.

Ray's contribution to Carmarthen Grammar School for Boys was immeasurable. It's no exaggeration to say that he had an influence on every teacher and pupil while he was there. He would be so proud when saying which teacher or ex-pupil had contacted him to wish him well before a big game, and would especially sing the praises of any teacher that would contact him.

A few years ago I came across a website about the history of the school, and this was written on it:

Carmarthen Grammar School was a selective secondary school built in 1576. Among its distinguished former pupils are educationalist Griffith Jones, Methodist leader and Bible publisher Peter Williams, senior Admiralty civil servant Sir

Walter David Jenkins, the clergyman James Rice Buckley, and rugby player Ray Gravell.

In over 400 years of history, Ray Gravell was amongst the five most esteemed ex-pupils of Carmarthen Gram.

Rugby Players

Clive Rowlands

Well, I remember Grav's first cap. I was the chairman of selectors at the time, and Grav won his first cap out in Paris in 1975. Now then, at the start of the weekend I thought to myself, what the hell have we got here, as he was singing Welsh songs one after the other. I remember that Saturday morning as I came downstairs to breakfast, and there he was – ready for the match at breakfast time! That was the kind of person he was, he was all heart, but he had a hell of a rugby brain on him as well. But what I remember most of all is Grav singing Dafydd Iwan songs on the bus all the way until we reached the stadium. Then, in the stadium, all the boys were having telegrams from Wales and beyond. But the one who had the most telegrams was Grav. He had more telegrams than the whole of the rest of the team put together! And suddenly there came a scream! 'Oh, look, I have one here from Gwynfor Evans!' But the most important one was saved 'til last. 'Oh, this one, this one is the most important, this one's from Mami and Toodles the cat!' By this time he was crying. The boys from Pontypool had never seen such a thing in their lives! So I took him into one of the small shower rooms to prepare him for the game. He was so ready for the game, dying to get on the pitch. And he had a great match, I have to admit. But Grav was Grav. He loved singing Welsh songs as loud as he could, and he had a decent voice, fair play!

I was very lucky to be out on a Welsh tour in Australia with Grav in 1978. Believe me, I learnt a lot about everything with Grav on that tour, but one memory stands out. In Australia, before the games, the mayor – for example the mayor of Sydney – would meet the players and shake hands. Then the mayor of Brisbane would meet them and shake hands. So, as team manager, I had to accompany them and introduce them to the players. So I introduced Derek Quinnell, 'Derek Quinnell', and he'd respond, 'How are you? Nice to meet you,' bla bla bla. And then Grav. Every time his greeting would be, 'Shwt y'ch chi heddi te?' (How are you today then, in Welsh) and the mayor would turn to me and ask, 'What did he say?' and I would have to translate every time! Throughout the tour he would do this, and I asked him, 'Grav, why do you have to do that?' Grav's answer was, 'You have to understand one thing. If France were playing here now, and Jean-Pierre Rives was speaking to them, do you think he would speak to them in English? No, he wouldn't. He would speak to them in French, and I will also speak to them in Welsh, every time. If they don't understand me, it's up to them.'

That worked for him you see. It was part of his life; it prepared him for the game itself. Players prepare for their matches in different ways, but Grav was unique. He had a special way of 'being ready'. You could nearly see his heart beating, he was so passionate! I think he hit the French player that was standing next to him in the tunnel before that first cap in France! And, as I said, he had a marvellous game and Wales won. What more can you ask of a player than that, that he gives his all from the moment he leaves Wales to the moment the final whistle goes out in France against Jacques Fouroux's team. And, of course, for him the cherry on the cake was the win for Wales and winning his first cap.

But you know what, he was a good friend to me. We could talk easily to each other, so naturally, without holding anything back. Both of us saying what was on our minds and able to be straight with each other. He was such a genuine guy. He would phone me nearly every day after his radio programme on Radio Cymru. 'How was the voice today?' 'The same as yesterday,' was the answer I'd always give him. 'Oh, right, right, right, I had to check up with you.'

He had Ceri Wyn Jones, the poet, on his programme once. He'd played in the centre for Wales Secondary Schools as Grav had. And Ceri wrote a poem which I read from time to time, as I'm very fond of it:

Pan fo'r glaw yn curo'n drwm
When the rain is falling hard
A rhaglenni'n radio'n llwm,
And our radio programmes are bad,

Yr un gân i'n cais ni i gyd,
We all ask for the same song,
O na byddai'n Grav o hyd.
Oh, that it was always Grav.

I remember JJ Williams scoring three tries in one game against Australia. Who was playing inside him but Grav. His strength as a player was his strength in a way. Not only his strength of body – he was very strong – but mental strength also. It worked for him to prepare himself for a game the way he did. It wouldn't have worked for me as preparation – it was his way. He also had skills when he played rugby. What people forget is that he was a scrum half when he played as a schoolboy, and he had those skills. Everyone saw him as a crash ball merchant. No, there was a lot more to his game than that, even though he was the best around at the crash ball. Somebody once said, 'Grav loves soft centres'. But I'll say it again, there was a lot more to his game than that. Grav and Roy Bergiers were the best pair of centres around in those days.

Gerald Davies

I knew about Ray because Mynydd-y-Garreg was only about two miles away from where I lived in the village of Llansaint. Even though we were brought up quite close to each other, I can't say that I knew him at all when he was a boy. I didn't really get to know him until he came into the Welsh team. When he started playing for Wales there were three of us

21

from the same school, Carmarthen Grammar School for Boys. That's when I got to know him well.

Some people felt that he was a very nervous person, but I didn't get that feeling when we were all in the dressing room. He was full of life and full of passion every time. Like everyone else, the first thing that comes to mind about Ray is the singing! In the dressing rooms and showers there was a huge echo, and that always enhanced his already loud voice. At that time the song he enjoyed singing was 'Carlo' by Dafydd Iwan, a satirical song with Prince Charles as its subject.

Carlo yn chware polo heddi,
Charles playing polo today,
Carlo, Carlo yn chware polo gyda dadi...
Charles, Charles playing polo with daddy...

Because he was so full of emotion, passion and mischief, I never got the impression that he was nervous, or was worried about the game. The impression I got was that he couldn't wait to get out there and for the game to start. He loved singing Dafydd Iwan songs and 'Carlo' is the first song I remember. A few years later he would always sing 'Yma o Hyd', which is now the main anthem of the Scarlets at Parc y Scarlets.

When he was on the pitch back then, I remember how there was always something worrying him, and usually it would be something to do with his health. His health was very important to him. In fact, it was quite an obsession with him. He would also worry about his standard of play during a match. I remember us out on the field playing an important international for Wales against one of the main opponents, and Wales were playing very well. He turned to me, because I was on the wing outside him, and asked, 'I'm doing alright aren't I, Gerald? I'm OK, aren't I?' He always needed reassurance that he was playing OK. 'The problem you see, Gerald,' he added, 'I've got this cough. I think I've got a cold, and I believe I'm coming down with the flu.' Now, all this was happening on the field during an important match for Wales, and I can imagine Bill McLaren commentating and saying something like, 'And there's the mighty Ray Gravell, the Viking. The bearded Viking in the Welsh midfield, powerful and strong, the opposition will have to watch him today!' That's how Bill McLaren would see him, but on the field Ray was worried that he might have a cold and was coming down with flu! That was part and parcel of Ray's character – there was a huge difference in how people who didn't really know him perceived him as a personality or character, just as Bill McLaren described him as the 'bearded Viking'. But, even though he was worried about his health and things would always play on his mind, when the ball was in his hands, Lord above, who was going to stop him? Or, when the ball was in the hands of his opponent, look out! As I said, that was part of his character, a dear and genuine man who could get on with anybody, and everybody could get on with him.

Being present at Ray's funeral was an unforgettable

experience. That is the closest I can remember to a state funeral in Wales. It was unbelievable. I came up to Stradey Park in the car on that day, and the streets were full of people wanting to show their respects to him after the service in the Stradey. The town was full. Thousands of people, and then, on the way to the crematorium, well... the streets were still black with people, some even standing on roundabouts. It was all absolutely amazing and unbelievable.

I felt it a true honour to have been invited by John Hefin to pay tribute to Ray at the funeral service, and I am so glad I did it. I must admit that I was worried, because when I do something like this there can be a moment in the tribute where one loses control of their emotions. I was determined to avoid this as I was delivering the tribute. I looked at the words while disconnecting with their connotation and significance, as I had already connected with the words while writing them. I just had to narrate the words while trying to avoid the emotion. But I raised my eyes at one point, and I knew where Mari, Ray's wife, was sitting, and I caught her eye. I really had to control my emotions at that point, and I slowed down and took a pause, and then carried on.

I will never forget that day. I remember Stuart Gallacher, who was chairman of Llanelli at the time, saying that it was so similar to how things were with Princess Diana, with people putting flowers on the gates of Stradey Park. He later told me,

'Last week, there was this quite elderly lady who walked

up to the gates to put some flowers down, and I had to go and see her, talk to her, and I said,

"That's very kind of you."

"Oh yes, well, I had to come to show my respects to a wonderful, wonderful man."

"Where are you from?"

"Oh, Bangor," she said.

"You've come down today?"

"Yes, I've come down today. I wanted to put some flowers here."

"Did you know him?"

"No, no, no, I didn't know him. I only listened to him on the radio and watched him on the television, but I didn't know him. I never met him.'"

Stuart Gallacher said that she had travelled down from north Wales to put flowers in memory of Ray on the gates of Stradey. I believe that many people felt the same, that they had never met him, that they had never shaken hands with him, but that they had gotten to know him through his personality and character on the radio and television.

Ray was so generous, so genuine, and everybody felt they knew him. He was the same with everybody he met, whoever they were. It was as if he was meeting an old friend, and he made everyone feel important and special after being in his company. He was a kind soul who was always interested in people – who they were and what they did. Whoever they were, the person that would be lucky enough to meet him would always be the centre of his attention.

Gareth Edwards

Well, of course, what comes to mind when you think of Ray is that he was a fantastic rugby player, he loved singing, yet there was this uncertainty about him, but I wasn't always convinced that it was uncertainty every time. It's difficult to explain because he was so confident in many ways. One thing he craved more than anything else was reassurance and confirmation that he was good enough to play for Wales. I don't think he could believe that he was there on the field representing Wales, and also that he was there with his heroes, because he was a little younger than us.

Before an international weekend we would train on the Thursday, and Grav would be full of it, but we didn't have much time to train for the match. Clive Rowlands and John Dawes didn't have time for any antics or playing around. They would often shout, 'Come on now Ray, get on with it!' because half the time Ray would be singing or shouting, 'Ohhh... hei... hup!' He was a tonic, but he could also be a little annoying because he would never stop.

Then, just before the game, and even during the game, he would come up to me and say, 'You like me don't you, Gar? You're fond of me aren't you, Gar?' And I would answer, 'Of course I am Grav.' 'Ohhhhhh, yes, pop it up Benny. Give it here, give it here!' It was as if it would fuel his strength and passion when he was reassured. Only one word, one little gesture, and I could see from his smile how he changed, not into a monster but into a powerhouse on the field.

In the dressing room before a game, Ray would be going

round singing 'Carlo, Carlo, Carlo…' especially before a match against England. I can remember Gerald Davies turning to me with a smile on his face. We were sitting there, putting on our boots, preparing for the match in our own way. I would be quiet, thinking. I wouldn't say much. I can remember Gerald saying to me, 'Gareth, if the England team came into our dressing room now, do you think they would be scared of us, or would they think we were off our heads?' There was Grav, preparing for the match in his own way by singing at the top of his voice, punching the walls, and barging against the toilet doors with his shoulder. In a way he was lightening the mood and making us smile, because Grav was on his own, a one-off. That was his way, and of course we would fuel it by praising him, saying things like, 'Well done Grav, well done. I've never seen you looking better!' 'Ohhhhhhhh!' Then we would open the door and he would go out on the field like a wild bull!

One game stands out for me. Wales against Ireland in Cardiff, and a lot had been written about Mike Gibson, Ray's opponent, in the papers. And why not; he was one of the best players at the time, an established Ireland and Lions international. He was an amazing player, outside half, centre, anywhere in the backs. They had been writing in the papers that Gibson would create problems and that it would be a difficult experience for Ray Gravell 'against the mighty Mike Gibson'! Well I'm sure, after reading this, Ray wouldn't have slept much for a week. During the game he came up to me as usual, 'Gar, Gar, you like me don't you?' 'Grav,' I said, 'of course I do. I've never seen you play so well!' 'Ohhhhh! Benny, Benny, Benny, hwp it up, hwp it up here Benny!' Phil Bennett then gave him a short pass and Ray ran through about four Irish players and knocked them over like bowling pins! It was as if he'd had a surge of strength from somewhere, incredible power from being praised. Things like, 'I've never seen you looking so good; I've never seen you look so fit; I've never seen you looking so strong.' 'OHHHHHHH!' He had one of the best games of his career against Ireland that day. People would look at us with disbelief if they knew that this kind of thing was going on in an international match.

Following that match against Ireland, on the Tuesday there was a Cup game between Cardiff and Llanelli. As I said, Ray had just had an amazing international, and one of the reasons was because I had built him up by saying how fit he looked. It was written in the papers after the Ireland match, 'The credit for the score should go to Ray Gravell who put down Mike Gibson with a ferocious shoulder charge.' He was now so confident and on top of his game. We were ready to go out onto the field for the Cup game. Cardiff, whom I played for, against Llanelli, and Ray came up to me, all smiles saying, 'Oh how are you Gar boi, alright? How are you Gar?!' That's how he was every time. And at that moment, completely unplanned, I turned to Grav and said,

'Bloody hell, what's happened to you?'

'What do you mean?' answered Grav.

'What's that pot there, what's that belly you've got there?'

And he looked down at his belly.

'What do you mean, what d'you mean?'

And with that, the referee shouted, 'Right out you go boys, onto the field.'

Grav and I ran out onto the field. He went one way and I the other, and I turned round and he was still looking at me with his hands out as if to ask 'what do you mean?' I put my hands on my belly, gesturing big belly, pot belly. I didn't think much more about it, just innocent banter. Well, Ray was having a terrible game: knocking the ball on, giving penalties away. I couldn't understand what was wrong with him. He knocked the ball on and from that scrum we scored a try.

In those days you would stay on the pitch during the half-time break, regrouping and talking in a circle. While we were talking, I had this feeling that there was someone behind me. I turned round, and there was Phil Bennett, slowly creeping closer and closer to me in the Cardiff huddle. And he said to me, 'Gar, Gar for God's sake, tell Grav he's not fat. He's driving the boys mad with it!'

Grav had been going up to Phil and JJ Williams (JJ has told me this story so many times) saying, 'Phil, Phil, I'm not fat am I? Gar says I'm fat!' I honestly hadn't planned it, I hadn't said it to try and upset him or as a tactic, I wouldn't have been able to think that quick! It was just banter, pulling his leg as it were, as we did as mates. If I'd said the same thing to Phil, he would have probably said something like, 'Oh I had a couple of pints with the boys,' and forgotten about it, but typical of Grav, typical of Grav.

We went to Stradey as favourites once. Cardiff were playing really well at the time, and I remember that Phil had told Ray about Paul Evans, who played at centre/outside half for Cardiff. 'Grav, oh, I heard them talking, I heard the Cardiff team talk as I went past their dressing room, and Paul Evans was saying he didn't rate you at all, thinks you're unfit,' winding Ray up like a corkscrew. Well, in the first tackle he floored not only Paul Evans but half of the Cardiff backs in one tackle! He was so wound up that someone had said – not just thought – that he was a soft touch! The boys knew how to wind him up, and then he would play magnificently. It was part of his character, and channelling his enthusiasm was the most important thing. When you whispered the right thing into Grav's ear, you could see him change, just like the Incredible Hulk!

Ray was unique, a giant, a friend, and I miss him immensely.

Phil Bennett

The story the boys always love – and the players that played at the same time as Grav – was the one about Bert Peel who was our trainer, Dwayne Peel's grandfather, you know. He was a real character, a miner, and he and Grav, oh, they were always at it, because Grav used to always tease him. We'd go in to do some weights, you know – we had a weights room down there – and Bert hated weights more than anything in the world. He believed, as a collier, that a miner or a farmer was strong enough by just doing their daily work. He and Grav, as I say, were great friends, but they were always having a go at each other and having a laugh afterwards.

Once, we were playing a match against Bridgend. Hell of a crowd, packed house there, and Grav was opposite Steve Fenwick and some very talented players; JPR would have been playing as well. Roy Bergiers was the other centre with Grav. Roy was a wonderful centre, made a beautiful half break on the halfway line, slipped it to Grav, and Grav caught the ball quite beautifully, went out towards JPR, drew him, and put JJ in, who flew in from about 30 or 40 metres for a wonderful try. The crowd went absolutely berserk and they were cheering JJ on the way back.

And Grav, I don't know if he was jealous, or just wanted attention. Grav was Grav, you know. Down he goes in a heap on the floor, screaming in pain. A couple of the boys ran up to the ref, and Bert had to run about 60 yards, and he was worn out running 60 yards to treat Raymond. He bent down and I came over, and Ray was writhing in agony and swearing in Welsh. Bert started rubbing some lovely white lotion cream all over his forehead. Grav went berserk. 'What the hell are you doing, Bert? Ma'r blydi boen lawr fan hyn, ychan' [the pain is down here], and Bert said gently, 'Yes, but Raymond, here's where the real problem is, up here.' And Grav was shouting and his language was red, and I was hysterical. Bert was so cool about it. 'Here's where the real problem is, Raymond. Lan fan hyn, myn yffarn i' [up here].

I can remember another story with Bert. We were playing Cardiff, which was a big game. Swansea was the local derby but Cardiff was *the* club; they regarded themselves as the greatest. We were playing Cardiff at Stradey, and I remember Grav came in that day, 'Oh, I'm not feeling well; I've got a headache, I can't play today.' There were no subs in those days. We were thinking who the hell could we get now, and I was saying come on, and the boys were saying, 'Dere mlân, Grav' [come on, Grav].

'Oh I've got a headache. I could have a brain haemorrhage; you never know what could happen.'

My God, he was driving us all nuts you know, and Bert was saying to him, 'Dere 'mlân y babi. Be sy'n bod arnat ti?' [Come on, baby. What's the matter with you?]

'Bert, bydda i'n bwrw ti nawr!' [Bert, I'll hit you now!]

Oh, what a build-up to Cardiff, Gareth Edwards and all these stars in their side. And I can remember, there were only 20 minutes to go before the game. We had two rooms in those days, the dressing room where we changed and the other room where Bert had a bench, you know, old-fashioned, where Bert would rub you down, massage you, brilliant trainer. He'd done my legs. 'Do me a favour and put a bit of Deep Heat on my back.' Suddenly Grav came bursting through the door. 'I'm going to go home.' I said, 'Oh Grav man, just give it one chance, please Ray, we need

you today.' Then I said, 'Oh Ray, will you try this thing for me?' He looked at me puzzled now. 'Beth, beth... what do you want?'

Brendan Foster, the great long-distance runner from Newcastle, was a great friend of mine, and he was the sports development officer to the whole of north-east England. 'Well you know, Ray, I told you I was playing for the Brendan Foster International XV on the Thursday.' So, to cut a long story short, I asked Grav, 'Grav, will you try these? Brendan gave me two or three pills, they're from America. He's been running in America, and these are the greatest pills for athletes that's ever been found!'

Grav loved pills and medicines. So I said to Bert, 'Bert, give him one, will you?' Bert looked at me as if he was saying 'what the hell are you talking about'. He went into his pocket, and I swear to God he said to Grav, in Welsh, 'Close your eyes Raymond, and put your head back a bit.' He put this pill into his mouth, and I said, 'Suck it now.' Grav said, 'Ew, nice taste to this pill, Bert.' I said, 'Ray, these are very expensive.' And he chewed it – this is true, honest to God. He chewed it and I said, 'He only gave me three, they're from America, new pills.' 'Duw, my headache's gone,' he said. He smashed the door, went back in to change, and he was ready to play Cardiff. I was hysterical and I said to Bert, 'Bert, what the hell did you give him there?' 'Well,' he said, 'you dropped me in it, give him a pill you said, and I gave him the only thing I had in my pocket which was an orange Tic Tac, so I put that in his bloody mouth.' So Grav had chewed this Tic Tac and thought it was some magic pill from Brendan Foster and his headache had disappeared, and he was ready to kill Cardiff! Oh, he was on his own, you couldn't make it up.

Isn't it amazing that this young shy man, when he grew older, would go on to act in films with famous actors and have his own radio show in the morning. He would always call me to say how the ratings were going, asking 'Are you switching on to me now every Tuesday and Thursday?' He'd phone all the boys, 'Remember now, 10 o'clock Tuesday or 10 o'clock Thursday.' I can remember him phoning me – on my children's life now – to say, 'Tune in Phil. I've got this lady, she's a very famous lady, she's an actress, she writes books or something, she's from America, flying in, and

I've got an interview with her.' And I'll tell you who it was: Jackie Collins, sister of the actress Joan Collins. 'Oh, she's bringing a new book out Phil, something about Hollywood; all of them carrying on, having affairs everywhere, there, this, that and the other.' So, I was listening in my car. Well, I nearly crashed the car. 'And now we hand over to Ray who's doing the show. Just come into our London studio is Jackie Collins, the famous writer who has a new book coming out.'

'Hello Jackie, are you alright?'

'Yes, nice to talk to you, Raymond.'

'Are you happy here, are you all settled in?'

'Yes, but I must admit, the only thing I'm missing is my cat,' Jackie Collins said.

Now Grav loved his cat, Toodles.

'Well Jackie, you've got a cat? I've got a cat too. Now tell me, with what do you feed your cat?'

Then they chatted about cleaning the cat, did it moult, did it lose its fur?

'And what about her in the night? I've got a cat flap you see, and she comes in and out...'

Well, they went on about the cat for about 15 to 20 minutes, and then he said, 'Jackie, it's been lovely to talk to you, all the very best.' Not a word was said about a book, not a word about Hollywood, not a word about anything but cats. Then Ray said, 'Mam, Jackie's got cats.' He knew his mother would be listening in Mynydd-y-Garreg. Well, I was hysterical. The boys were phoning me up, 'What the hell

35

was that? He's absolutely mad. I know more about cats now than I ever wanted to!'

And he phoned again, 'Tune in this Thursday. I've got this great man.'

I love cricket and he had Fred Trueman coming in.

'Oh Ray, I saw him playing at St Helen's. He's a great England cricketer, a wonderful man from Yorkshire. I always remember him.'

'Oh, welcome to the show Fred, welcome to the programme.'

'Well yes, Raymond, we're very much alike, you down there in west Wales with your collieries and us up here with our coal.'

Ray's father was a big miner, you see.

'Duw, you have coal up there? What coal have you got, Fred?'

'Anthracite.'

'Duw, we've got anthracite down here now. How would you burn it? Do you put some "cols" in with it? ... How long does it last with you? ... How much coal do you mine out of there?'

Well, honest to God, 20 minutes on coal, how to burn it, how to use it and everything, not one word about his wickets, how many he'd bowled for Yorkshire, how much he'd bowled for England.

Back to the rugby, and you'd know your music well when Ray was playing for Wales. We only had two toilets in the Wales dressing room. They were nice changing rooms, but only two toilets. Grav used to go in with a programme, lock the toilet door, and he would be in there for about 45 minutes. The Pontypool front row wanted to use the toilets, and all they could hear coming out of the toilet was this song, 'Carlo'. Dafydd Iwan had brought it out, and Ray was singing it at top of his voice. I can remember Charlie Faulkner, who couldn't speak a word of Welsh, being livid saying, 'Who's this *&^%$ Carlo, who's Carlo, who's Carlo, Phil?' I said, 'The Prince of Wales.' 'Jesus Christ!'

He'd come out of the toilet then, and I can always remember there was a huge mirror, and he'd go and look in the mirror, put his chest out, and he'd have the three feathers there you know, and he'd rub the three feathers. Oh, and you know what, I'd swear he'd have half a tear, and sort of think about his mother and obviously his father. But

for about 45 minutes you'd have 'Carlo' to work him up. And then, he'd look at his chest, look at the three feathers and get ready for it. I can remember the Pontypool front row – you know Pricey never said a crossed word to anybody all his life, just shaking his head as if to say, 'Where does he come from?'

Ray was on his own. It was a privilege to know him and a privilege to play with him. What a man, what a player.

Simon Easterby

I remember in the early 2000s, Grav was obviously a constant presence at Parc y Strade, whether that would be working for S4C or supporting us as president of the Scarlets. I vividly remember one day, turning up for a Saturday evening game, and myself and Sarra at the time were on a short break in our relationship. Well, Grav collared me before I even made it into the changing room, and told me how wonderful Sarra was looking earlier on, as he'd just seen her, and I just remember his words...

'Ohh, Ohh, Ohh Sarra! Ohh Simon! ... Ohh Ohh!' He couldn't really go into more detail than that, but I knew exactly what he meant. He was trying to convince me that Sarra was looking beautiful when he'd seen her earlier that evening, and what was I doing having a short break from going out with her.

It didn't stop there. I went into the changing room and, as Grav always did prior to a game, whether he was working at the game or whether he was just there supporting us, he'd always come into the changing room to wish us good luck. Obviously, he was meant to be impartial when he was working there, but he was always true to his colours and would be supporting us through thick and thin. But that day he made a point, probably about five minutes before kick-off, of coming up to me again and saying how wonderful Sarra looked when he'd seen her earlier and that, basically, in no uncertain terms, we had to get back together. It was a pretty difficult match for me afterwards, with everything going on in my head about the game, and obviously thinking about Sarra and what Grav had said. I think we won the game thankfully, but it was a bit of a strange one for me, and one that I will never forget. Grav had a big part, I think, in myself and Sarra getting back together not long after that. That would be one of my many memories of Grav as he was obviously, as I said, a constant around the club and in our lives for a good period while I was there, from 1999 and right through until he passed away in 2007.

What I remember about his funeral is pretty vivid in terms of the outpouring of grief from people that knew him, people that maybe had just shaken his hand, or even people that hadn't had the good fortune of meeting him in person. He touched everyone in a special way but also, I think, he touched people in different ways. He was one of the only people that you'd meet who always made you feel like you were the only person that he'd spoken to that day. He was so full of enthusiasm, and never short of a word of encouragement whatever you were doing. He'd offer a confidence boost. Wherever he was, he was always there to support, and to say a positive word about the things you were doing. It was really tough to be a bearer at his funeral. It will forever stick in my memory as something that you would never want to have to do, but obviously it was a huge honour when myself and a number of the then current Scarlets, and ex-Scarlets, were privileged enough to carry him on to the ground prior to the service.

I think, when you saw the number of people that were at the funeral, who were all there showing their respect to Grav, it just hit home what he actually meant to people. But, ultimately, after the doors were closed and everyone was back in their own homes, one felt that he should never be forgotten. He was not only a great man, but also a great dad and a great husband. He is missed by everyone, and I can't believe that it's over ten years since his passing. I feel very fortunate to have had him in mine and Sarra's lives, and the fact that he was able to celebrate our wedding with Mari, his wife, was wonderful. It was probably testament to the encouragement that he gave in making sure that we got back together.

Ollie Campbell

As a starter, I'll just say that the doyen of all New Zealand rugby writers, Sir Terry McLean, once said of the Lions, 'they have a magnetic attraction', and I think you could say exactly the same thing about Grav, he had a magnetic attraction. He was a wonderful man and a hell of a player too. It was a privilege and even a blessing to have known him.

The first time I met with Grav was in London, at the hotel where the Lions had gathered for Bill Beaumont's 1980 tour to South Africa. He came over to me and welcomed me, and he said that he was delighted to meet me. He said, 'I hear you're quite shy,' and then he added, 'I am too,' before disproving this in the days, weeks, months and even years ahead. So that was my first meeting with him. My last connection with him was, actually, only a few weeks before he passed away. I gave him a call, as I did from time to time, and he answered the phone as he always did and said 'Seamus', because Seamus is my first name (I was christened Seamus Oliver Campbell), so he always called me Seamus. So I said, 'Conas tá tú?', which means in Irish 'How are you?' And straight back came 'Tá mé go maith, go raibh maith agat' which is, 'I am fine, thank you.' Spoken like a native Irishman! So that was my first meeting with him, and my last connection with him as well.

I have an image in my head. We're at Newlands, Capetown; it's 1980, the first Test, and he's coming on. I'm in the stand, he's coming on. He's on the side of the pitch doing his warm-up before coming on as a sub. He seems to have done, from a distance, a very passable impression of Tarzan! He was certainly beating his chest, and it looked like he was shouting just like Tarzan would have done in the jungle. It's just an image. I never asked him about it, but that's one of the images I have from that tour.

During the second Test I came on with about 15 minutes to go. So, we're in Bloemfontein, in the Orange Free State, and this was my first Lions Test. So, it's 16–15 to South Africa and there's 15 minutes to go, and the game is in the balance. What you would normally expect would be a 'Congratulations!' from the centre outside you, maybe a 'Good luck', maybe a 'We have the winning of this game, just give me the ball.' Instead of that, Grav came up to me, looked me in the eyes, absolutely seriously, and said, 'How do you think I'm playing? Do you think I'll get selected for the third Test?' So I reassured him that he was playing brilliantly, and he would be the first name on the team sheet for the third Test. He was very happy with that and we got on with the game.

We were playing the Orange Free State. Grav had made a tackle on his opposite number, De Wet Ras. This happened in the first play of the game, and was so late it was almost posthumous! It went unpunished and unseen by the referee. Interviewed on the TV afterwards he said in all seriousness, whilst explaining what had happened, that he had been told from a very young age to get his first tackle in early, even if it was late! That was the beginning and the end of the interview.

I have one final memory. The Lions were playing against Northern Transvaal, which was really the fifth Test, at the famous Loftus Versfeld Stadium in Pretoria. Grav couldn't find his gum shield! And he made it clear to the team that he would not be playing unless his gum shield was found. So, as Grav wandered around this huge dressing room, singing along to Dafydd Iwan on his Walkman, and being sick in the toilets, the rest of the Lions searched the room high and low in gear bags and blazer pockets for his gum shield, some even on their hands and knees. Eventually, Grav found it himself. It was in his pocket! 'Sorry boys' was all he said, as he continued with his routine of singing along at the top of his voice to Dafydd Iwan, and alternatively being sick in the toilets.

Grav was like an onion. There were so many layers to him. And every layer was good too. It's said that to be forgotten is to die twice. Grav will never be forgotten.

Bill Beaumont

Well, really fond memories of Grav. I didn't really know Grav before the 1980 tour to South Africa because, you know, playing in the north of England, I didn't play many games against him. At that time of course Grav had been in the Welsh side, and everybody appreciated what a character he was.

I remember we all met up at a Heathrow hotel on the eve of the Lions tour to South Africa, and he was so, so excited, really, really excited to be part of the Lions. And he used to call me Bo-Bo. He always called me Bo-Bo for some reason.

He was just one of the guys; he was just infectious, yet he really needed reassuring all the time about how he was playing. Whenever on the field he would always be at you, saying, 'Am I doing alright? Am I doing alright?' You'd say, 'Of course you are!' because the last thing you'd ever want to say to him was 'You're not', because he would worry about it! I think a few of the lads used to wind him up, saying, 'You've not had a great game today, Grav', just to see what his reaction was. There's all the old stories about his nerves and him saying: 'I've got to get my first tackle in early, even if it's late!'

Being his captain, he was a what-you-saw-is-what-you-got, straight up-and-down, tough hard guy, crash ball, smack-it-up-all-day, really! But he was probably a better rugby player than people gave him credit for. You know, you don't play for the Lions, and you don't play for Wales or in those great Llanelli days without being able to play. You know, he could play, without a doubt. And in the modern game, which requires a lot of straight runners, he would be able to name his price, he would that. He was a very strong, abrasive runner.

I never shared a room with anyone on that tour. As captain I would always get a separate room. So I never got to share a room with him, fortunately! At the time both of us were smokers, something I am not proud of. We used to get three cigarettes given to us, and I always remember Grav would draw his cigarette and he'd look at me and say 'Tosted', referring to the tobacco (toasted rather than sun-dried), but all he would say is Tosted! I'd say toasted, and he would say Tosted.

I was fascinated by his passion for the Welsh language, and he obviously was very much a passionate Welsh Nationalist, in a nice sort of way. In a nice way, you know, he would make you understand his passion. And this carried on in later life of course, with the Eisteddfod and things like that, where he was very much a leading light.

After the Lions he didn't play in the 1981 Wales v England game, and I wasn't involved in the 1982 game and we both retired from international rugby that year.

There was a funny incident when we'd both retired. It would have been 1983, February '83 when I used to do a bit of work for the BBC on *Grandstand*. The story goes that S4C were doing their first-ever broadcast of a live match (Wales v England), and Grav was one of the co-commentators. They were rebuilding at the Cardiff Arms Park, and we were in a sort of a Portakabin, really pitch-side, really right on the side of the pitch! And I remember Grav just came in and was sort of chatting away (live on air!). I understand he almost delayed the broadcast by his late arrival for the debut on S4C! But, I believe he rescued it by telling everybody that it was the first rugby international broadcast in the Welsh language on S4C! I think he used his 'get out of jail' card there.

My last conversation with him was in October 2007, and it was an hour before England played South Africa in the World Cup final (20 October). He rang me up on my mobile, and he said to me, 'Bo-Bo, I never thought I would do this, but I'd just like to say I hope England win today!' and he added, 'I was suspicious of England and of the England players, but in 1980 [on the Lions tour] they were all good lads.' And he did get on really well with myself, Fran Cotton, Peter Wheeler, Clive Woodward – we all got on really well together. We lost him just 11 days later.

He was just an infectious guy. Everybody liked him, everybody loved him! He's one of those people who wouldn't have an enemy in the world. There's no one in the world of rugby that wouldn't say that Ray Gravell was a good guy.

Delme Thomas

I remember the first time I got to know Ray. I went on the Lions tour in 1966 and Ray was at Carmarthen Grammar School at the time and I remember meeting him when I came back. Then he came to play for Llanelli at a very young age, he was under 20 years old. We became friends from day one, difficult to explain why. Maybe it was because both of us came from a village background, country boys with the same interests and delights. I'll never forget his first season playing with Llanelli. He'd come to Llanelli in his small green MINI. I would get into this MINI; well, you could see the road where you put your feet! How it passed its MOT I'll never know. I was always pulling his leg about the MINI. It would break down all the time. I remember going up to Swansea one evening and it was pouring with rain, and the car would break down every two to three miles! He turned to me and said, 'This car doesn't like rain, it doesn't like wet weather!' I would have to push it then, to get it started. Oh, I pulled his leg about that car.

I remember going to South Africa with Llanelli in the early 1970s. Of course, it was very different out in South Africa then, with apartheid and all that. I remember staying at a hotel in Johannesburg, and Grav and I were sharing a room. I remember telling Grav, 'Now listen Ray, don't you leave your money about the place here. Look after your things, because the Africans, well, they don't get paid a lot, and you might find one or two things going missing.' And that was that. I shouldn't have done it, but, the next evening I hid Ray's new trainers under the mattress of his bed. He got up the next morning, and we were going out to train, and he couldn't find his trainers of course. Well, there was a hell of a fuss, and I told him, 'I told you to look after your things.' And that was that. We went to bed that night, and very early in the morning they would bring us the daily papers and put them on the dressing table. I heard the door open, and Grav jumped out of bed and grabbed this poor guy by the collar and shouted at him, 'Where's my training shoes?' I had to tell him quickly where they were! And to the day we lost him, he laughed recalling that incident and when he found out that I had hid his shoes.

Another story. This is from before the time he played for Wales. Ray was always complaining about his health, that there was always something wrong with him. His leg was hurting, or his back was painful, or he had a headache. Bert Peel was the sponge man with us at that time in Llanelli. Everybody knew what Ray was like, and were asking what was wrong with him that day. When we went on the bus to play somewhere, all we'd hear was, 'Oh, boys, I've got a headache!' 'Oh, boys, my back is killing me!' Bert Peel would give him tablets. Different coloured tablets for whatever was wrong with him. They weren't tablets at all, they were Smarties! Everybody would know that they were Smarties, but Ray thought they were tablets, and he would say that they worked, and he felt better.

And I'll never forget a match at Stradey Park. In the final two minutes of the game he had a smack on the leg and had to go off. At the end of the match we all went into the dressing room, and there he was lying down on the treatment table with Bert Peel rubbing his head. Ray said to Bert, 'Bert man, it's not my head that's hurting, it's my leg.' 'I know,' said Bert, 'but here's where your problem is!'

Oh, he would come into the dressing room and we were all trying to prepare, and he would be singing Dafydd Iwan songs at the top of his voice! He would get on everybody's nerves. When Carwyn James would talk about the game, the tactics, and stalk our fires for the game ahead, he would run to the toilets and be physically sick. He would be so nervous before every game.

When I was captain he had to be second out onto the field behind me. The boys had twigged this, and there they'd be, pushing him back, further and further back, pulling his leg of course.

I'll never forget him telling me about his father – he lost his father at a young age. Poor lad, I'll never forget him telling me, just after it happened, because we were very close, on that very day. His father had gone out with the dog, a little terrier, and of course his father didn't come home. He went out to look for him, and he could hear the dog barking by his father's body. I remember him telling me, it was very hard. We were very close, and even after I retired from rugby (I was nine years older than Grav, so I retired years before him) he would come here to see me every Sunday night.

The thing about Ray was that he could talk to everyone, no matter who they were. If you were a tramp or a down-and-out, he would want to talk to you. And I believe that was the reason he was so popular, you know. There were no airs and graces with Grav – what you saw was what you got with Ray, and I miss him so much. We shared the same birthday, and when I first told him he didn't believe me, he was so made-up that we shared a birthday! He was here with me about a week before he died, and I couldn't believe the news when it came that he had gone. Everybody was affected; even talking to people today in Llanelli, Grav still comes into the conversations often. A huge loss. What a man, and what a Welshman!

John O'Driscoll

Well, it was on the 1980 Lions tour to South Africa that I first got to know Ray well, I didn't really know him before that. I bumped into him a couple of times, and for some reason we just became great friends right from the beginning of that tour. Neither of us were in the Saturday side in the first couple of weeks, and then eventually we both ended up in the Saturday side for the Test matches. We had a week's holiday, if you like, when there was no match. We went to a nice holiday resort near Durban, and we asked if we could share a room for that week.

The third person – there were three of us who used to pal around a lot – was Maurice Colclough, God rest his soul. It's very sad really now. I remember, Ray and myself met up quite a few times to go and see Maurice when he was dying. Maurice was living in Swansea and he had a brain tumour. So I would go over and Ray would pick me up in Cardiff and we'd go to see Maurice. We went to his funeral together and we saw a lot of each other at that time. It was also so sad when Ray died because, unlike Maurice, it was so unexpected.

Ray had a Celtic affinity, there's no doubt. He liked the way of life in Ireland, and he especially loved the music. Music was so important to him. He was amazing in the dressing rooms before matches, you know. He'd suddenly burst into song. Ah, it was great stuff.

I also remember he liked to be reassured about things. He's the only person in rugby I really had chats with on the field during matches! I mean, the Test matches in those days were every bit as tense as they are now. The Lions Test matches against South Africa were very intense, but Ray would come over for a chat during the match! Nobody else did it before him, and nobody else afterwards. I can remember in the third Test, after about 20 minutes, there was a scrum, and Ray comes over to me, and I thought he was going to say something about, you know, tactics or something. 'Hey John,' he said, 'Hey John bach, you're going well, you're going well. How am I doing, how am I playing?' And I replied, 'Oh, so-so.' To this day I can remember him wandering back to his centre position, laughing and saying, 'Bastard, bastard!' He also made me his personal doctor on the tour. He always had various minor ailments.

West Wales and home were so important to Ray. Everywhere he'd go he would say 'West is best, West is best!' That was his motto in life. We just had wonderful times together. I saw a fair bit of him, and then, you know, you're busy with your life, with work and everything. I always thought, well, I'll see a lot more of Ray as the years go by, and then suddenly he's gone before we really got down to doing that. He was an unusual combination of hardness and gentleness. Great empathy, great sensitivity. The simple fact is, when you were wandering around with him, having a few pints with him, the whole time he was just a joy to be with in every way.

Family and Close Friends

Mari Gravell

Ray was no DIY expert at all. One Christmas, when the girls were very young, we got them a trampoline. He'd been really looking forward to putting this trampoline together, and he wanted me to help him.

So, along came Christmas Eve, and it had gone quite late by the time we got started putting this trampoline together, it was gone 10pm. It was very warm in the room, and Ray was dripping with sweat putting it together. But, fair play, he had placed everything in an orderly fashion, and he knew where everything was, and I was his assistant. We took over two hours putting it together, and making sure the tension of the mat was right and that everything was in the right place.

As we were clearing up, Ray stood up to admire his work, and was so proud that he was able to do this for the girls. He knew they would be over the moon as this was one of the big presents they had asked for. Yes, he was very proud. As I got up to my feet and was collecting

the rubbish, I noticed that I had been sitting on a bag of washers that were supposed to be used with every screw in the trampoline! Well, I was scared to tell him what I had done, but I had to admit it in the end. He wasn't very happy, because we had to re-do everything and add these washers to every screw! But, in the end, the result was great. The girls were over the moon in the morning, seeing the trampoline in place, and they were so proud of their dad, that he was able to help put it together.

*

Manon's birth, the first baby. There was only me, Ray, and Vicky the midwife there. Ray came into the room and started asking questions.

53

'Right then, Vicky, where's the gown, where's the gloves? What am I supposed to wear? Where is everybody?'

'This is it, Ray. Me, you and Mari!'

'Oh, I thought there would be a lot more than this here,' he said.

It took ages before Manon was born. I was exhausted, and all I could hear was this music playing and everything was getting on my nerves. Anyway, things started to move, and were coming to a head, but for some reason I just couldn't push. I was so tired; I had no energy at all. Then Ray said,

'Come on now, Mar. No pain no gain!'

Well, I couldn't believe it. I didn't know what to say. I couldn't believe that he'd said such a thing, and I shouted at him, 'Get out of the way, get...!'

And Vicky said to him, 'Hey, come on now Ray, come on now. That's a bit out of order isn't it, Ray!'

When Manon was born I was a little shocked because, you know, in the end she just came out. Well, Ray was in floods of tears, and he went to sit down outside the room and a doctor came to see me. One of the other doctors went to Ray and asked him,

'Are you alright?'

'Yes,' he said, crying his eyes out. 'I've just had my first baby!'

Gwenan was seven weeks early. So, a completely different story. We were up in Caernarfon on a Sunday morning, because Ray was recording some quiz programme – I can't remember the name of it. We were staying at the Celtic

Royal Hotel, and we were going up to our room, but they had given us a room with no bed for Manon, even though we had asked for a family room. 'Oh, no problem,' they said. 'Someone will come and help you with your baggage now.' So Ray and the porter were carrying the bags and Manon and I were walking behind them. Out of the blue, I became ill. I don't know what came over me, but I couldn't put one foot in front of the other. And Manon asked, 'Are you OK?' But I couldn't speak. Manon started shouting 'Dadi, Dadi!' and Ray turned round and saw that I looked terrible.

'Bloody hell, what's the matter?' And I could only whisper, 'I don't know, I don't know.' By the time we reached the room I had a massive headache and I had to lie in bed with blankets over me. I couldn't make out what was wrong with me. Anyway, we had to call the paramedics, and when they came and saw me one of them said,

'We better take her to Ysbyty Gwynedd.'

'Wow now,' said Ray. 'Wow now. I can't have a Gog baby up here. We'll have to get the air ambulance to take her down to Glangwili Hospital. Do you understand this? Now then boys, I'm not trying to be funny or anything, but I can't have a Gog baby!'

But, thankfully, the sickness went as quickly as it came. We went home once he had finished recording the programme, and I was fine on the Monday. The midwife came to see me and said that she didn't think that it was the baby that caused it. But, by Wednesday morning, the same thing happened again, and this time the baby was the reason behind it. It all happened because there was a tear in the placenta, but we didn't know that until she was born. So in we went. We left home around 8.30 in the morning, even though I don't think Ray thought I was in labour. But, by the time we reached the outskirts of Carmarthen, he started believing me and he even started overtaking on the inside to get us there quicker. We arrived, but then it took ages for us to see the specialist, Mr Roberts. They took me up to the ward, and Mr Roberts said, 'Jiw jiw, you're going to have this baby today whatever happens.'

I now thought I was going to have a caesarean. Mr Bloomfield was the specialist with Gwenan, and this time it was as if they were selling tickets for the birth, where with Manon there was nobody. This time it was packed full of students, doctors, nurses, because it was a different birth to the norm.

So then Ray noticed all this and he turned to Mr Bloomfield and said,

'I better go now, I better get out!'

'You stay where you are,' he said to Ray. 'She's going to need you now!'

In the end, in a matter of minutes, Gwenan came, she was out. Well she was only four pounds, and she was purple. And Ray said, crying buckets again,

'I've kissed one end of her, but I'm not sure which end it was!'

And they took her away. But everything was fine, even though she had to stay in hospital for three weeks.

When Gwenan was small, Ray had an event in Llanelli he had to open or something.

'I can't take her with me,' I said, because I was working.

'I'll take her with me,' he said, because it was an event which had something to do with children.

So I said to him, 'All her clothes are here. So you dress her when you're ready, and make sure she's fed before you leave.'

'Right, yes, yes, no problem, no problem.'

Well, whatever had held him back in the house, he was a little late leaving and he had to rush to get to the event on time. So he must have driven like hell. When he got Gwenan out of the car – she was around two years old I think – as he picked her up she vomited all over him, all over his suit and everything. But, as luck had it, the event was being organised by one of our best friends, and there were a lot of women there to fuss over Gwenan, and some of them went at it to clean her up, while the others cleaned Ray up before the event started. This was all so typical of Ray, so typical.

*

The year before we lost Ray we went to the same place as usual for our holidays. It was my cousin's house, and all we had to do was book our flights online. The year before, we received a piece of paper as confirmation with all the names on it. Great. But things had changed the following year. They were not sending out any paperwork. All we had to do was put the flight number in our phone and that's it. Well, the night before the flights he was full of panic. And he said,

'No, no, I want that piece of paper. I'm not leaving here if we don't have that piece of paper with us.'

'Listen, we don't need it,' I said to him.

I had to phone this guy, Joe, who worked at the Scarlets, and he would come round here to sort anything out to do with the computer. I knew that Joe went to Scotland regularly to see his parents. Joe had said to me, 'I always book online now. I'm not going to bother with any papers.'

Around 10pm the night before the flights, I phoned Joe. 'Joe, can you explain to Ray, will you, about booking tickets online?' Jo explained to him, but Ray wouldn't believe him either.

Our friend, Dai Penn, was taking us to the airport. Ray said,

'Right, I'm not going to allow Dai Penn to go home until we know that we can go on the flight. Really now, I don't think we'll be allowed to fly without a piece of paper or anything to show them.'

He barely slept a wink all night because he was so worried. He would wake up and tell me, 'I bet you know, there'll be a bloody fuss about this tomorrow.'

'Ray, please, just go to sleep will you!'

On the journey to the airport Dai Penn also told him, 'Listen now Ray, they've moved on, it's the 21st century now Ray.'

'Dai, please now, don't leave us until I know. I'll go to the desk straight away, and then I'll tell you if you can go back home.'

By the time we got there the queue to the desk was out of the door. So at the airport I said to Dai, 'Listen Dai, just go.'

While we were in the queue waiting our turn, Ray was still at it about the blinking piece of paper. We eventually arrived at the desk and, as it happened, the lad on the desk was from Bridgend, and the first thing he said was,

'Oh Ray, there's great to see you going on holidays. How are you feeling? Are you better?'

'Yes, good thanks. Now listen, I'm a bit worried,' said Ray. 'Last year when we came here we had this piece of paper with all our names on. There's nothing this year!'

'Well, you don't need anything any more,' he said. 'Have you got the number?'

'Yes, I've got the number here,' said Ray.

He zapped the number. 'That's all we want.'

'Well, bloody hell,' said Ray, 'I didn't sleep at all last night thinking that I wasn't going to get on the plane to Spain!'

Once he knew that everything was fine he changed completely. He was so worried. His insecurity was the reason behind it, poor dab.

He was the same with the mobile phone. No interest in new technology at all. He just wanted to be able to use the phone to call or answer someone, and to read texts. That's all he wanted to do. He had no interest in sending a text; he'd rather have a chat.

He used to hate airports. We went to Hong Kong many times, going out to seven-a-side tournaments, and he'd usually go with a group of people as a 'tour leader' with Gullivers Sports Travel. Everyone would want to talk to him, and he would be in his element talking with all of them. The last time we went he had gone a week ahead of me because we'd had Manon by then and she was only around 18 months at the time. He had gone to China for a week, and we went out to Hong Kong to join him there. We arrived in Hong Kong and the plane wasn't able to land because the weather was so bad. Storms! It was awful! We had to turn around and around in the sky for ages. Manon had been great on the flight, sleeping just in front of me in a little cot. I had changed her already, because Ray had told me that everyone would be waiting for us. All he had been talking about I can imagine, even in China, would have been Manon! By the time we landed she'd been ill and had vomited all over me and I didn't have any other clothes to change her.

When we arrived at the hotel, oh my God, everybody who had been with him in China were all there waiting for us like some sort of welcoming party! After such a stormy landing I looked so pale. As we arrived he came out to meet us both, full of enthusiasm and excitement, and I told him, 'Please, take me to our room. We've had a journey from hell.'

But ask me he did, 'Have you been drinking?'

I could have belted him one, and I said, 'No, we've had a horrible journey.'

He hadn't registered that the storms were the reason for the delay.

'But everybody's here waiting to meet you!'

I went past them all, shouting, 'Shw ma'i pawb. Hello, how are you all? I'll be back now,' before making a beeline for the room.

I couldn't believe it. Oh, have you been drinking? For goodness sake! He was just so excited to see his family arriving.

*

Ray's mother was in a residential home in Mynydd Mawr at the time, having had a stroke and needing care. We couldn't look after her. We had planned to go and see her one Saturday, and the night before Ray had said, 'Oh, we'll go and buy a ring tomorrow!' He never asked me, or proposed or anything like that, just said, we'll go and buy a ring for you.

'Oh, right then. Oh, great,' because I knew exactly what I wanted. I had seen one years earlier, before Ray was on the scene even. I knew what I liked. So, we were on our way back now, after seeing his mother, and we came down through Llanelli. But, instead of turning into town, he turned the other way onto the road that would take us home. Well, my heart sank. I thought, oh, flipping heck. That's it now, that's it. And he asked,

'What's the matter with you?'

'Nothing, nothing...'

'What's the matter? Oh, bloody hell, the ring!' he said. 'Oh, bloody hell!' And he did a U-turn there and then, and went back to buy the ring.

I didn't want a big fuss or anything when we got engaged and, as it happened, that's how it was. So we talked then about getting married. Again, I didn't want a huge fuss. There was a lovely hotel in Mynydd-y-Garreg, and we were going there and having no more than 40 people to the wedding, and that's that. That's what we had agreed and arranged. In the meantime, Ray was off to the Philippines to film *Filipina Dreamgirls*, and he was there for some six or seven weeks. He would phone every day. He spent all the money he was making on the film on phone bills! One night, he was on the phone. I can't remember what the time difference was, but it was the early hours of the morning, and he said,

'Have you done something about the wedding?'

'Yes,' I said. 'All done, 40 people, as we agreed.'

'No, cancel it. I want more than that.'

'No, no,' I said. 'That's what we agreed.'

'No, I can't. I know more. I'll have to ask more than 40 to come to the wedding. So cancel it.'

'No, I'm not cancelling it.'

He came back and cancelled it, and we then had a carnival instead of a wedding. We had around 180 people in the end.

Oh my God! But it was a great day. Roy Noble said of the wedding, 'It was a three-day event!'

Gwenan Gravell

My story is more embarrassing than anything else. It was one of the first times we went to McDonalds with Dad. We had done the car thing before, the drive-thru, but we hadn't actually been in. So, we went in, and I can remember going down to the counter, and for some reason the guy said, 'I'll bring the food over to you.' So we had ordered everything, and went to sit down. So he came with the food, and Dad asked, 'Oh, do you have a wine list? And what about a knife and fork?' Manon and I were, of course, dying of embarrassment! Then the guy said no. Dad said, 'You don't have a wine list? You don't have a table cloth?' And we were thinking, Oh please shut up Dad. After we got home we told Mum. 'Oh my God, Mam, we're not going with him to McDonalds again!'

Another thing I remember. When I was at primary school we went to see a panto, one of Dafydd Hywel's pantos, I can't remember which one it was. All the schools were there, everybody sitting next to each other. I can remember about halfway through the panto Dad just walked in, came up to us, and sat with us. And I can remember at that time, because I hadn't really noticed it before, how everybody knew Dad, and I was thinking, how do they all know him? I remember just sitting there and all these kids running towards him, and

I thought, why is everybody so obsessed with my dad? He's just my dad! I was just so embarrassed, because it hadn't happened before, or I hadn't actually seen it before. I was thinking, we're in a panto, why are you all...?!

Manon Gravell

I'd been to the Urdd camp in Llangrannog on a school transition course with Ysgol Bro Myrddin's Year 7. The weather was really cold. I came home and there was this kind of huge rash around my mouth because of the weather and it being so cold. As we arrived back from the transition course, I didn't really know all the other children well, but I knew I would be spending the next seven years of my life getting to know them, and becoming best friends with them. The first thing that happened after we got off the bus was meeting Dad. In front of everybody, with these huge red lips because of the cold, Dad asked in his loud voice, so that everybody could hear him, 'Who have you been snogging then?' In front of everybody! I didn't know where to put myself! I thought, 'Great Dad. Thanks Dad! Ideal for a girl in her first year at the school!'

When I was 11 or 12, I had just arrived home from school and Dad was watching the races on the telly – as he would often when I came home from school. I walked in through the kitchen and he said,

'Oh, Mans, come and sit here for a minute. I want a chat with you.'

So I leant against the radiator, and he said,

'Right, right… now that you are in secondary school, I have to have a serious chat with you.'

I thought, 'Right, OK.'

'Now then, I'm going to tell you about the birds and the bees, and all you need to know is that the birds fly on top, and the bees fly underneath.'

And that's all the chat was!

'There you are, off you go!' and he went back to watching the races. I thought and thought about it, and I asked him, 'What am I supposed to do with that information, Dad?'

'Oh, you'll understand when you're older.'

And I still don't understand what he was on about!

*

Dad and I were obsessed with seafood. I remember when Uncle George (Mum's uncle) was sick in hospital, Mum went to see him one night, and said to Dad,

'Right, I've put the oven on, and I've bought you some dressed scallops from Marks, and all you have to do is to put them in for half an hour and they'll be ready.'

'Yea, yea, good. Ta-ra, ta-ra, ta-ra.'

So Mum went. Dad put the scallops in the oven while I was watching telly and not taking a lot of notice. He pulled them out, and said, 'Right Mans, food's ready!' I wanted to see the end of this programme on telly. He shouted again, 'Right, come on, food!' So I went to eat, and I didn't notice or didn't think why the food was cold. I didn't think much of it because I blamed myself for leaving it so long before eating it. Anyway, Mum came home and walked past the oven and said,

'Oh my God it's hot in here. The oven is still on.'

And Dad said, 'No, I'm sure I turned it off.'

He looked at the oven and said, 'Oh my God, I put the food in the wrong oven!'

So we had eaten the scallops raw! Dad went into panics and shouted dramatically at Mum, 'I've killed her, I've killed Manon. I can see it on the front page of the *Western Mail*, saying that she died and "Ray Gravell kills his own daughter!" and things like that.'

One of my godparents was a doctor, so Dad phoned Martin and said to him,

'Martin, Martin, I've killed Manon!'

'What? What?'

'Well, I haven't killed her yet... but she's eaten raw scallops!'

And Martin asked, 'Well, does she feel OK?'

I said that I felt fine, and then Martin didn't think it would have any effect on me.

Mum asked me, 'Didn't you notice that the food was cold?' And I answered, 'Well I thought that the bottom of the scallops was warm. So I just thought that I had taken so long to get to the table and that it had gone cold when I ate it.'

But I was fine, and that's my attempted murder story!

*

When we were out in Australia, well I reckon that Dad and I ate between us twice our body weight in seafood! Dad made sure we went to all these posh restaurants to eat, because Gullivers were paying. They would give us 'the best experience'. One night, Dad and I were at this seafood place and there were live lobsters available there. Dad and I went to choose a lobster, and I chose one that looked rather 'sedate' and Dad said,

'No, no, she'll have this one,' and it was bound to be around seven kilograms of a lobster. It was enormous, filling up the whole tray!

'Do you expect me to eat all that myself?' I asked.

'Well, I'll help you if you get stuck.'

I didn't get stuck, and I ate it all, and Dad was really gutted that I managed.

*

Once, I was on the way home from school, and Dad was at home by himself. This was after he had had the 'op' on his leg. Dad was hopeless with his phone, useless! He could read a text and make a phone call, and that was it. So, I was on my way home from school, and I got this phone call off Dad. He sounded quite strange on the phone. I asked him,

'Are you OK?'

'Yes, yes, I'm fine. Listen, I've got to go.'

'Well, OK.'

'Nothing's wrong, just hurry home. Right, ta-ra.'

And I thought, 'Oh my God, what's happened?' So I belted it home, and Dad was there in the middle of the kitchen, in his chair, saying,

'DON'T MOVE!'

'What's the matter, what's wrong?'

The cat had walked into the house with this massive slow worm in her mouth (Dad was petrified of snakes), and he didn't want to make a sound in case the cat let it drop on the floor. It was as if he was trying not to scare the cat, but the chair would squeak every time he moved. So he was trying to roll himself out of the room in his chair, but the cat was following him and getting closer and closer, because the chair was making this noise.

'Dad, what do you want me to do with the cat?'

'Just take her out, quick.'

'Right, come on Celt. Out we go.'

As she was going out, the slow worm around her neck was going nuts! It was horrible! And Dad was shouting, 'Out with her, out!'

*

He didn't like things that flew either, and neither do I. When I was born, this bat came into the room. Because it was hot and the middle of summer, all the windows were open in the hospital, and this bat flew in! Mum was protecting me to keep me safe, and Dad was running around the room like a banshee shouting,

'Get it out! Get it out!'

He caught the bat in the corner with a bin. Then he got hold of it, even though he was petrified of flying things, and threw it out of the window. He could be brave when he needed to be.

Nanette Jones

Well, there are so many stories about him. I remember once a robin flew into my house, and I'm not too keen on anything like that. I phoned Raymond for help.

'Don't worry,' he said. 'Tough toenails, I'll be down to see you now.'

Well, I don't know who was more afraid – the bird, me, or Raymond! Everything went haywire. There were more screams coming from Raymond than from the little bird!

I remember another moment, and that was at a special wedding. To cut a long story short, on the night, Mari had gone to bed. There was only Raymond, me and Martin left. When we eventually decided to go to bed we noticed that the hotel's door was locked. So where was he going to sleep? With us? Did I mention sleep? Between Martin and Raymond snoring, I didn't sleep a wink. I sat in the chair all night. So that was a long night!

Sarra Elgan

About a week after Grav had seen Simon at that game (check out Simon Easterby's tale) – when Simon and I were separated and having a break in our relationship – he came on a TV show I was working on with S4C at the time, called *Noc Noc*. On the show we visited the homes of young viewers and filmed live from different rooms in the house. I was presenting the programme with Rhodri Owen. Grav was one of the guests, and I'll never forget him coming into the lounge of the house we were in that week.

'Oh Sarra,' he said. 'I saw Simon last week, and he was devastated. He was absolutely devastated!'

I didn't think he was devastated at all to be perfectly honest, but that's what Grav said to me, 'He was devastated!' And another thing Grav said to me, 'Think about the babies,

Sarra. Think about the babies. Half-Welsh and half-Irish. Perfect mix! Perfect mix!'

He was a very special person. He had the ability to make everyone feel fantastic, and if he felt something was right he was determined to make it work. And that's what he did with Simon and me, and by now I'm so glad (obviously! haha!) that he interfered.

It was lovely to have Grav and Mari at our wedding. It was very special for us, and we told this story at the wedding. So we have a lot to thank Grav for.

Elin Hefin

Around 35 years ago, John and I lived in Cardiff, in Treganna. Ray was busy and at the peak of his powers. During that time Ray would go to Radio Wales every day. He would hate leaving Mynydd-y-Garreg and Carmarthenshire, but he would still come to see us every day. Being on Radio Wales, talking to people from all walks of life, I believe, taught him a lot because he was like a sponge, taking everything in. He was quick, and very clever. He hadn't been to college, but heck, he was so quick and witty.

John and I had just married in 1985, and Ray was half living with us. That in itself was a lot of fun. We were all heavy smokers at the time, and liked a drink too – smoking Irish cigarettes and drinking Irish whiskey as if it was going out of fashion.

Before long I was expecting and, as the months went by,

Ray was taking more and more interest. 'El fach, El fach, El, El, El,' and I would answer, 'Yes, I'm fine, yes, yes.' I'd been reading books, as you do when you're expecting a baby, and I'd read somewhere that in the last stages of giving birth your legs go cold, apparently. Well, he had to have this idea. 'Right, I'm going to give you a pair of socks that I wore for Wales. You can wear them, El. You'll be fine then, great!' So that's what happened. I wore them, and Meg was born between two red socks.

He gave things to everybody. I believe he gave away every international shirt, his caps. He gave a pile of rugby shirts to some rugby club, I can't remember which one. The club closed in the end, and they found some of Ray's shirts in the attic, but Mari got them back eventually. He would give away Lions blazers to people. He was just so kind. He was so generous with his time and with his care for people. We went out for meals often, the three of us, and John was also very generous. Before the meal would end the two would make excuses to go to the toilet, or slip a card to the waitress, and it would always be a competition about who was paying, not who was going to avoid paying.

Ray could also be insecure. We travelled a lot with him to London. When I was producing *Jabas* in north Wales, John and Ray would come up to stay for the weekend. He would come to Borth with us frequently, too. He would talk with everyone. But, if he came across someone with the attitude of 'Who the hell are you?' or a little stiff, well, off he'd go; he'd be determined to get them to talk with him. I remember being in London with him, and we were standing in this queue to phone John. John was off somewhere with work, and there was this woman behind us in the queue, poker-faced. 'Don't bother Ray, don't bother,' I said to Ray. 'You won't crack this one!' But, without fail, he would get the stiffest of people to laugh.

There's one story that I think is quite revealing and true of his character. When we lived in Borth, Aberystwyth would attract a lot of the Jewish community every summer. They would stay at the university and have a holiday. Jewish societies from all over the UK would come. There was no problem with this at all, but it was very difficult to interact with them, even to say hello. I remember being on a train from Birmingham once, and moving so that they could sit together. No thank you, no acknowledgement, nothing.

We were all sat on the decking one day in Borth, looking out at the sea. There was a family of Jews sitting together on the beach. 'Ray, forget about them. They really keep themselves to themselves. Quite arrogant in a way.' 'Oh?!' Ray was on one leg by then and using crutches. I can see him now, going down to the beach, across the pebbles, and up to this family that was just sitting there. And we were sitting on the decking watching him from afar and thinking, he's going to do it, he's going to succeed. In the end he had these people eating out of his hand. We were still on the decking when they came past us as they were leaving, and usually they would have completely ignored us. But they came up and leant against the fence so they could chat with us all. He'd done it again! Yes, there was insecurity in a way, but there was this huge confidence too.

Back to the '80s and, as I said, he was half living with us. I remember someone once coming round to the house to wax my legs. I was upstairs, lying down, and this girl was waxing away. The phone rang. It was Ray, and I said, 'Oh, hi Ray.' (I was determined not to tell him what was happening because…) 'El, El! What's the matter?' He was very sensitive. As the girl was waxing and I was getting tenser, my voice was changing as the pain hit me. Not that I was making a noise, but he sensed that there was something not right with my voice. Well, he was convinced that someone had broken into the house, and that someone was trying to do something to me. 'I'm coming down there now. I'll be there now,' he said. He was at home in Mynydd-y-Garreg at the time! 'Ray, sorry, I'll have to tell you then. I'm OK, I'm having my legs waxed.'

He was OK then!

Janet Rowlands

When our girls Sioned and Sarah were little they, along with Manon and Gwenan, were obsessed with *The Teletubbies*. Us parents as well, on the hush-hush, also started to get obsessed with them! All the children wanted to have the complete collection of Teletubbies, and everyone was looking for these toys in shops like Toys "R" Us and places like that. The demand was so great that there weren't any available in shops in south Wales.

Well, Dafydd Rowlands (the Archdruid of the National Eisteddfod of Wales at the time), my father-in-law, was going out to Ireland with the Gorsedd of Bards to some meeting. It became a family mission now, for both families, to try and find a Laa-Laa. Well, Dafydd went out to Ireland, and between two meetings in the company of Jim Parcnest I believe, they went around the toy shops of Dublin asking if they had a Laa-Laa! After about two days, phone calls came from Ireland, one to me and one to Mari and Grav.

'Don't worry,' Dafydd said, 'we have found a Laa-Laa.' And back from Ireland came two Laa-Laas, one for the Gravells and one for us. Therefore, the two sets were complete and everyone was happy. Grav's reaction was typical. He was over the moon and all excited, like a wild man, thanking Dafydd for spending his precious time with the Gorsedd roaming the streets of Dublin looking for a Laa-Laa. Of course, we were not allowed to forget this for many years to come. The Teletubbies, and especially Laa-Laa, had pride of place in Brynhyfryd from then on.

One night the Gravells came round to ours. We had ordered an Indian takeaway. The place we live, on The Graig, is a little remote, and we had ordered a delivery from the Indian restaurant in the village. We had phoned at seven. 'Right, yes, it will be with you in half an hour,' was the response. Half past seven came. Nothing. Eight o'clock and not a sign of them, and there we were still waiting.

By this time the wine was flowing, but even then we were starting to get fed up with the waiting. Half past eight. Still nothing. So I gave them a call at around a quarter to ten.

'Look, where is the Indian we ordered for half past seven? Where are you?'

'We're on the way, we're on the way, we're on the way! We think we have found you.'

So Grav got all excited now that the food was here, and we were all starving! We had a balcony out the front on the second floor, so out went Grav onto the balcony. It was a very dark night, clear and very quiet in Craig-Cefn-Parc. The next thing, Grav saw a light coming up the road. He shouted,

'The Indians are coming! The Indians are coming!' and that was the welcome for the takeaway at our house that night.

We used to go away a lot as two families when the girls were small, and I remember one time we went towards Evesham and Stratford, because that's where the land of the Teletubbies was. And I remember how we used to always eat out, either at the hotel or at lunchtime at whichever place we fancied. There were six of us then with Manon and Sioned, but Gwenan and Sarah hadn't been born yet. I think Mari and I were expecting at the time. We would walk into any hotel or restaurant, and it would always be Grav who would ask for a table, and it would always be the same line everywhere. He would say, full of pride in his huge voice, 'Table for six please, and two high chairs!' And that's how it was until it became, 'Table for eight please, and four high chairs!'

Mansel Thomas, Mynydd-y-Garreg

I have so many memories of Ray.

There was a concert in Mynydd-y-Garreg to raise money for the Fron Intensive Care Unit at Llanelli hospital. I remember Ray bringing a print of Meirion Roberts' work to the auction. It was a very famous print of Carwyn James and the Llanelli squad that beat the All Blacks. The print was sold for £200. The person who bought it was Ray himself, and at the end of the concert he presented the print to Simon Holt, the breast cancer specialist in Llanelli.

*

It was a Saturday afternoon and Llanelli were playing against Swansea. The two wings for Swansea were Arthur Emyr, the Wales wing, and Tony Swift, the England wing. Before the game, Ray thundered his way into the Swansea changing room. He looked around and shouted his greeting, 'Arthur Emyr and Tony Swift – you call yourselves wings? I've seen better wings on a bloody blackbird.'

*

There was always something wrong with Ray. We were both filming in a Trefdraeth pub for *Darn o Dir* one day. He was convinced that there was something wrong with his ear.

'Mans, Mans, look inside my ear will you. Can you see something?'

'Bugger all, Ray.'

I had this all afternoon, the same thing, 'Look again will you, there must be something there.'

Looking into his ear all afternoon was starting to get on my nerves now. In the end I said, 'Good Lord Ray, everything is clear. I can see right through to the other side.' The ear was suddenly better after that.

*

Ray would be so willing to do anything to help anybody. Well, nearly anything. Mynydd-y-Garreg had a cricket team that played in a competition against other villages in the area. I asked him on many occasions if he would play for us, but the answer was always no. He would always come up with an excuse each time. But once, I pressed him and asked him why he really couldn't play. The answer hit me, 'I'm afraid of the ball.'

*

There's another story about him, live on Radio Cymru. Ray was presenting a show, live from the Llew Coch pub in Llandyfaelog. There was a dog called Henri in the pub, and he was famous for his singing. At the time there was a husband

and wife from the Netherlands – the wife being rather large – staying at the Llew Coch. The highlight of the item was having the dog sing. And fair play, Henri was in the mood and on form, hitting all the high notes. The lady from the Netherlands had lost it completely, and was overwhelmed while listening to Henri's heavenly voice. She slipped bit by bit down her chair and fell unceremoniously to the floor. Radio Cymru listeners had a colourful running commentary from Ray, describing what was happening, saying, 'There's a 'wompen' (wompen is a Welsh slang word for enormous) of a lady who's fallen on her arse in astonishment at Henri's musical talent!' She didn't understand Welsh, thank God.

*

On another Saturday, Bridgend were playing at home against Llanelli. Playing for Llanelli was JJ Williams. JJ had just left Bridgend, and was expecting a rather warm welcome from his old teammates. In the days before the game, JBG Thomas from the *Western Mail* had described Ray as the best centre in Wales. In the dressing room Ray was going around asking everyone if they believed that he was the best centre in Wales. But, during the game, Ray delivered a hospital pass to JJ. Poor JJ received the ball and a tackle at the same time. He was in quite a bit of pain on the floor. Ray went up to him, and the only thing Ray said to him was to ask the question, 'JJ, do you think that I'm the best centre in Wales?'

Eamon Duffy

I first met Ray during the amateur days of Leinster; there would be a pre-season Leinster v Scarlets game over the years. Then we became great friends, close friends, and best friends in 1987 when we were both involved with the first Rugby World Cup in New Zealand. He was working with a company called Gullivers Sports Travel, quite a well-known company. He was their Welsh personality, and I was involved from the Irish end. The tour leader from Ireland was a notorious, funny, and great character (also now passed), Moss Keane. I was sort of Moss' minder on the trip.

So Ray and I worked, in a way, together and then we became best friends, and we started meeting each other without any connection to rugby whatsoever, and our families were very interlinked. I became very close to Ray and his mother Nina (because he wasn't married to Mari then). I went back and forth to the 'Mountain' (Mynydd-y-Garreg, where Ray lived) from Dublin a lot. So I had a great relationship with Nina despite the fact that she was a very, very shy person, but I got the best out of her and Ray appreciated that. He was working at the BBC at the time. There were four in our relationship (Mari wasn't around in those earlier days), so it was Ray, his mother, myself and the fourth was Shamrock the cat! And Shamrock the cat was unbelievable, honest to God. I actually think that bloody cat could talk to him! You know, for a big man... and you'd see him with this cat! Oh Jesus!

In 1988, a long time ago now, the Olympics were held

in Seoul. The Seoul Olympics were quite famous for many reasons which we'll come to in a moment. I used to slip over to the 'Mountain' for a couple of days at a time, but this time I said I'd go for an extended period – maybe eight, ten days or whatever – over on the boat to watch the Olympics. But there was a problem with watching the Olympics at Ray's house. (This was before Ray had done a fantastic job in renovating the cottage on the side of the mountain into a beautiful home.) At this time it was small; there were only two bedrooms, his little bedroom and Nina's room. He kindly gave me his bedroom, which there was absolutely no need to, because I would have preferred to sleep down on the couch in the lounge for the simple reason that the actual Seoul Olympics were being broadcast to us in Ireland, Wales and the UK in the middle of the night, you know, and the TV was in the lounge.

He was getting up religiously at 5.30, 6 in the morning when he used to do a show on the BBC with Frank Hennessy, so therefore he needed his sleep. But the television was in the lounge where he was sleeping. So, believe it or not, myself and his mother Nina used to go into the room where he was sleeping to watch the Olympics. Now, we could sleep during the day, myself and Nina, while he would be at work, you know. So he would be grumpy, telling us 'please!', warning us 'please!' He'd be warning his mother as much as me not to wake him up, you know, by shouting that he wasn't interested, he had to get up for work at five. In those days, himself and Frank Hennessy used to do this BBC Roadshow which would take them out and about around Wales, and he would have to travel even earlier in the morning (if he didn't go the night before), but he would prefer to stay at home.

So, as you can only imagine, it was a very eventful Olympics with Ben Johnson, the Canadian, setting a new world record for the 100 metres, and of course a couple of days later he was stripped of his gold medal because of drugs. Of course, we, you know, woke up Ray so that he could watch the race with us. Now, I said to Nina, 'No, no, we'll leave him to sleep.' He was half asleep anyway, so I said, 'Let him sleep.' But she wanted me to annoy him as much as possible, you know, and the two of us were playing up. Now we shouldn't have done this, and it was pure devilment just to try and keep him awake, and annoy him more than anything else. And then, of course, we watched the Ben Johnson race itself and the brilliant world record that was set. Carl Lewis, I remember, was second in that race. And on another night we woke him up – I don't know if you remember Florence Griffith-Joyner, she was a multi-Olympic champion – for her sprint races. I remember another time, at about five in the morning, his mother had gone over to him and said, 'Raymond, Raymond, wake up. You've got to see, you've got to see the pole-vaulter!' Because this famous guy – his name was Sergey Bubka, a famous Soviet pole-vaulter – created a new world record. Ray had as much interest now as the man on the moon. He would go mad! We'd have to run into the kitchen, and he'd be banging the door, it was just unbelievable. But, what a character! Then, finally, later on during the Olympics, in the middle of the night when the news came through that Ben Johnson had been stripped of his medal, we were so excited, it was such big news that we said we'd have to wake up Ray. You'd think we were the devil's advocate waking him up, but we woke him up out of excitement, and of course he went nuts, you know. But, the funny thing about him was, how he had the patience and the understanding to allow us to do this, while at the same time he wouldn't go upstairs to his own room and use his own bed because I was the guest in the house. But it just shows you, we drove him absolutely bloody nuts, and he just played along with it, but that was the kind nature of the man.

Another part of that story was that he did fall out with myself and Nina on one occasion. On most evenings on his way home from Cardiff he would call in at the White Horse, which is a pub literally across the road from the old Stradey Park. There was a guy there who was like a father to him, more like a father to him than anybody else, Norman Gale. Ray called us on the house phone to say that, if we couldn't give him a commitment saying that we wouldn't annoy him that night by waking him up and acting the cod (as he was going up to north Wales for an outside broadcast) then he was going to stay at the White Horse with Norman.

So Ray didn't come home that night, didn't come home for the dinner that Nina had prepared for him, and that sort of laid down a marker to us, right there. So we were feeling bad about that, and you know maybe we pushed it too far.

83

But you know what, when he came home the next day he was all apologetic, that he was the one who had let us down by not coming home! You know, just such a beautiful man.

That man who played for Wales, he was a severe, ferocious competitor on the pitch, oh my God! There used to be the sign with 'Gravell eats soft centres'. That was a great one at the time. I don't think I ever saw a harder rugby player than Ray Gravell. But he was like, you know, such a baby, such a laidback easygoing guy off the pitch, unbelievable, unbelievable. I can't explain that to you as well as how it was; he was so tough on the pitch but such a soft personality; how he treated his mother, how he looked after her, how he watched over her and cared for her, such a petite little woman.

Another true story, because both men confirmed it to me. Ray was playing at Lansdowne Road, against Ireland, and there was a young Irish out-half only playing his second game for Ireland, a guy called Micky Quinn. I actually knew him because we were at boarding school together. Anyway, Micky was a fine player but of a very nervous disposition. He was in the era of Ollie Campbell and Tony Ward, but would have been slightly older but not in the same league as Campbell or Ward. There's very few that would be in the same league as them, you know. Anyway, Micky was feeling pretty nervous and uptight and was under the stand at Lansdowne Road for half an hour, 40 minutes, before the game kicked off. He was on the toilet, sitting down having a crap, and nervous as can be. In bursts Ray through the toilets' door (because the same toilets served the two dressing rooms in those days, you understand me? There were separate shower areas whatever, but the toilets were shared). So in bursts Ray, and of course he decides that he would like to have a 'number two' as well. So he goes into one of the cubicles next to where Micky was. Ray heard someone in the other toilet, so Ray starts to sing one of his favourite Dafydd Iwan songs, and you can imagine it would be rebellious and whatever, and in Welsh. Well, Micky Quinn said he nearly had a bloody heart attack! You know, sitting on the toilet, he couldn't get off the toilet he said he was that scared! And then Ray, you know, started banging and kicking the door as he sang the song. Ray said to me, 'By the way, I was only in there for a pee, but I knew there was somebody else there. I saw the boots underneath, and I wanted to let them know that I was there.' Anyway, he was shouting, roaring and banging the door and whatever, and Micky Quinn ended up having a bloody disaster of a game. It's a fact, because both men, both Micky Quinn, the out-half playing Number 10 for Ireland on the day and Ray Gravell playing 13, both men told me exactly the same story, not only separately but together when we met years after that.

He was legendary, and then of course he had a great love of Irish music. He liked the rebellious stuff, yes. He loved The Dubliners, he loved all that sort of stuff, and he loved Christy Moore. And Christy Moore is the biggest Irish folk singer, and he's in his mid 70s now. He's the Dafydd Iwan equivalent over here. Christy was telling me that when he came to the UK, he had a number of gigs in England and Scotland and then some in Wales. He always played in Cardiff. And whenever Christy was over in Cardiff, he used to absolutely one hundred per cent commit to contacting Ray directly about going on Ray's show at the BBC. It wasn't just to promote his shows because Christy Moore, with all the Irish people living abroad, could fill every hall. He'd fill every theatre or concert venue because he was extremely popular as you know, and still is a legend here. But he loved going on the radio with Ray, and the reason he loved it he said was 'because of the craic'. The fun with Ray, and having a laugh with Ray, a bit of a chat, and then, you know, depending what time he was on, if there was time for a bit of a lunch or whatever afterwards.

Ray had this touch, a special touch, he was amazing. Now Christy Moore was a busy guy, and was handled by his management very well over the years. He was extremely popular but giving TV and radio interviews wasn't easy for him, as he was very politically motivated and that sort of stuff. He loved Ray and loved Ray's Welshness and the fact that he was the carrier of the sword – a bard as well as being a legend on the rugby pitch, and off the pitch!

It was the same with the actor Richard Harris when he would come and visit his friend, the musician Terry James, in Kidwelly. He would want to meet with Ray for a pint and a laugh. The Furey brothers, Finbar and Eddie, very well-known folk singers here; The Dubliners' John Sheahan, Ronnie Drew and Eamonn Campbell (their guitar player), they loved seeing Ray come over for internationals or whatever. It's amazing the people that would just look forward to having a chat and a laugh with him, because he was so funny, so sincere. I never saw him walk down a street, whether it was in Sydney, Australia; Auckland, New Zealand or wherever, he'd stop and talk to everybody.

Finally, as an aside to all this, behind every great man is a great woman. Mari Gravell is probably one of the greatest women or people that I've had the pleasure of meeting. Meeting Ray Gravell and his mother Nina was fantastic, and Mari Gravell is equal to both of them. And his two daughters, Manon and Gwenan, are unbelievable. Ray continually sang a Welsh song to his wife about her being his anchor. All the time he sang it, morning, noon and night. He loved every inch of the ground that the woman walked upon, and she did him. It was the most amazing love story of all time. And thank God for the fruits of that, his two beautiful daughters.

To lose that man the way we did... I mean, I remember the *Western Mail* saying a day or so later that not only had Ray passed away sadly in Calpe in Spain, but that a part of Wales had also passed. And I actually believe that.

Commentators

Huw Llywelyn Davies

Onllwyn Brace was our boss when we started to broadcast rugby in Welsh on S4C, and he invited Grav to join the team. It was new territory to be full time on S4C then, and Grav was the obvious character, I think, to join us. He was fantastic for us in that period. He wasn't an analyser – he was never an analyst – he was just a fan, and he could transfer that enthusiasm to our listeners and viewers. He was so important in that period when we were trying to establish the service. Because he was so dear to everyone, he was a critical figure in that early success.

Onllwyn made him the offer, 'Do you want to join?'

'Of course.' Because he would love the camera and the microphone.

Then Onllwyn said to him, 'But, if you want to join us you will have to give up playing.'

And Grav asked, 'Why?'

'Well, you'll have to be unbiased you see, when you go on air.'

'But Onkers' – that's what he used to call him – 'Onkers,

Onkers, 485 games for Llanelli. Phil May is the only one who's played over 500. Please can I...'

But Onllwyn said to him, 'Grav, no.'

Both of them could speak Welsh, but Onllwyn spoke more English perhaps, and Onllwyn said to him,

'No, no. If you're joining us, you've got to finish playing. Because, from the start, I can't have people saying, why have they got a Llanelli player talking? But it's up to you.'

Then he said to Grav, 'Is it the BBC or Llanelli RFC who's likely to pay your mortgage?'

This was in the amateur days. And Grav said to him, 'Shows how much you know about the treasurer at Llanelli!'

But in the end he came on board.

I remember the first international we did, the first live broadcast. Grav had been very reluctant to give up playing. That was natural; he enjoyed the adulation and hero worship of the Scarlets and Wales. So, before the first game, and I remember it well, they were renovating the stadium at the time. It was 1983, Wales against England at the start of February.

'Grav! Right, I'll pick you up at the BBC,' I said to him.

No, we had to meet at the Angel Hotel, where the Wales team were staying of course, so he could be part of that excitement in the middle of all the fans. Then, walking across the road, we took about half an hour to cross Westgate Street, and down we went to the tunnel that was going to take us to the stand. Our commentary podium was at the other side, and there was nothing else there. There wasn't a stand, only a ladder, and a large box where they had put us to commentate. But, as I said, it was at the other side.

'No, not through the tunnel. No, we have to go in front of the crowd,' Ray said. So we had to walk around, in front of the crowd so that he could once again wave at everybody, and everybody of course recognised him. 'Duw, hello Grav,' everyone said. Then we went past this hut, where *Grandstand* was being broadcasted that afternoon. As we went past Grav asked,

'Who's in there then?' And I answered that I thought it was the Network broadcasting from there.

'Who have they got then?'

They had Bill Beaumont with them – Bill was Grav's captain on his tour of South Africa with the Lions.

'Oh, I'll just slip in there now to give Bill a wave,' said Grav.

'You can't mun! We're on air in a while.'

Everyone was quite nervous and Onllwyn was up in the box waiting for us, and we were all thinking how all this was going to work out. Was it going to be accepted and appreciated? Everyone was on tenterhooks.

Grav said, 'I'll be with you now in two minutes, Huw.'

I said, 'Come with me now Grav.'

'No, just going to...'

I went towards the commentary box, and up the ladder.

'Where's Grav?' Onllwyn asked.

I said that he just had to go somewhere for two minutes, and that he'd be with us now.

But there was no sign of him. Ten minutes, a quarter of an hour, 20 minutes went by, no sign of Grav. Onllwyn by now was going ballistic! We were around half an hour before kick-off, and the second voice still hadn't arrived. Onllwyn threatened,

'He's never going to work for the BBC again. Discipline, out of the window. Useless! Where is he?'

Onllwyn, by this time, was checking all the equipment and pushing the buttons on the monitors we had. Suddenly, what came up on the monitor? *Grandstand*. Who was in the *Grandstand* studio? Ray Gravell, with Bill Beaumont. Not only had he gone to wave at him, he had somehow worked his way into the studio, and once he was in there they had to interview him. Onllwyn went berserk!

But, typical of Grav, he arrived full of beans. Onllwyn was primed to give him hell but, before he had a chance, 'Onkers, Onkers, I've done it. I've done it. I've told the world we're starting on S4C TODAY!'

Onllwyn couldn't say a word to him then for arriving so late. He'd given such publicity to our programme.

Throughout the years, I've always said that there's a special relationship between a commentator and his second voice. The commentator excites and the second voice brings a little bit of sense by looking at things a little more objectively and tries to calm the commentator down. I think it was a completely different scenario between the two of us. He never did any analysis. That's why, in a way, after 20 fantastic years together, Ray moved to the touchline, because down there his enthusiasm was even more prevalent. That was when Gwyn Jones joined. The difference between Gwyn and Grav is massive, both brilliant in their different ways. Players would come out, some from all over the world, and they would see Grav, and S4C would get the interview before anyone else, primarily because of Grav's presence. Everybody knew him, everybody loved him. He was so honest and innocent in a way.

I can remember saying to him once during a Wales game when he was as one-eyed and biased as usual in his comments – everything was *we*. 'Oh, I hope *we* can get out of this now!'

I said to him, 'Grav, try saying Wales instead of *we*.'

'Why?'

'So that people think that we are rather fair to both teams.'

'@£$%&* rather fair?' he said. 'Rather fair? What do you mean? We're here, speaking in Welsh and @£$%&* Wales are playing down there. Is there anyone out there that thinks we support any other team but Wales?!'

He didn't once, in all the years that I worked with him, predict that Wales would lose. His verdict was, 'Well, I know that everyone thinks that... But I believe today...' and that was during a very poor and trying period in Welsh rugby's history.

I would always try and tell him to be more objective. But he'd turn up wearing a red shirt, or he'd have a red tie, or a red scarf. Onllwyn had to tell him in the end, 'Ray, you

know... Just so that you can look a little bit more impartial, don't wear red to the game.' And he turned up for the next game, in Paris, with no red in sight!

Onllwyn said to him, 'Grav, for once, you listened to me boi, thank you very much. Well done. I like that. Discipline.'

And Grav answered, 'Yes, Onkers, if you tell me boi...'

Right, we did the game, and out we went to do interviews. That was it, all finished, still thousands outside the Parc des Princes in Paris. But, Grav suddenly took his trousers down, on the pavement, outside the Parc des Princes!

'Onkers! Onkers! You didn't think I'd come here with no red at all?'

He was wearing a pair of underpants that were as red as anyone could find, in the middle of a street with thousands of supporters, his trousers down at his ankles, with a huge smile on his face.

Gareth Charles

I can remember Grav telling a story about one of his early caps, not the first one which he won against France, but the next game against them I think. France had a hell of a team at the time, and Grav was very new to the international scene. In the heat of battle he found himself at the bottom of a ruck, and who was there with him but Jean-Claude Skrela. Now France had a fantastic back row in those days: Jean-Pierre Rives, France's 'poster boy', Jean-Pierre Bastiat, so experienced and a huge man, a giant of a number eight, and then Jean-Claude Skrela. Skrela was the quiet one, but also the hardest one. Grav saw him on the floor and, as he's said many times, 'I don't know what came over me!' And what he did was, he put his two hands around Skrela's neck, choking him and shouting, 'Kill Frogie, Kill Frogie'. And all that Skrela did was just look up at him and smile. Grav took his hands away quickly and said, 'Only joking!'

I'll never forget the first time I went to Ireland, not just the first time I worked there but the first time ever. Wales were playing in Dublin, and because it was my first time there Grav had decided to take me under his wing and take me around one of his favourite places in the world. We went out on the Thursday afternoon. There wasn't a lot to do, no hourly bulletins or reports online, or social media like we have today. So we went to Baggott Street and into Foley's pub. I remember having a quiet pint there with Grav, and he asked the lad behind the bar if they had a phone. There were no mobile phones at the time of course, and he explained to him that he wanted to broadcast. It was Hywel Gwynfryn who was broadcasting in the afternoons on Radio Cymru at the time, and Ray needed to make a contribution to the programme. I'm not sure if Hywel himself knew anything about it, or whether the item had been organised beforehand, or if it was Grav who just wanted to do it. Anyway, we got a phone, and he had them call us back. So he was live on air with Hywel Gwynfryn, talking about everything being fantastic, and he had to put me on then because it was my first time there. So I also had a chat with Hywel live on radio. Great, and that was that.

Now then, there was a man standing beside us at the bar, looking very dapper in a three-piece suit. He asked Grav, 'Oh, what language was that?' and Grav answered, 'Cymraeg, Welsh'. Then, bingo, Grav and he clicked straight away. And as it happened, in a complete coincidence, he was a member of the Garda, and was the personal driver of the Taoiseach, the Irish Prime Minister. He had just finished his shift and had called into Foley's on the way home. He insisted on driving Grav and I around Dublin for the rest of the day. Grav wanted to go to the Brazen Head, the oldest pub in Ireland, and show it to me. He also wanted to pop into the Swan, because the landlord there was Sean Lynch, who had been with Grav on a Lions tour a few years before.

The Swan was in a rough part of Dublin. We parked outside, and this young boy came up with dirt on his face. The man who had been driving us around all afternoon in the prime minister's car said to him, 'This is the Taoiseach's car, so you look after it. Make sure nobody touches it!' He put some coins in his hand. And that's where we were for the rest of the day. We then had a party with the Garda that night as they happened to have one planned. That was Grav for you. He could establish a friendship with someone in the blink of an eye, and remember them for ever.

My favourite story about Grav as a broadcaster is when he and Frank Hennessy had a programme together on Radio Wales called *Street Life*. It was on in the mornings and a mixture of music and chat. They would have experts in their fields on the programme: money experts, gardening experts, cooking experts and medical experts. One morning, it was Grav on the mike, and they had a doctor in. They received a phone call from a Mrs Jones in Caerphilly.

'Now then Mrs Jones, the doctor is listening here. What is the problem Mrs Jones?'

'Oh, well, it's my son, my little boy, he is just two years old, and he... he's... he can't stop playing with himself. I don't want to tell him off too much. I don't want to hit him or anything, because that could have some psychological effect on him. I don't want to shout at him because I've heard that that could be traumatic for him when he's older. But he's just playing with himself all the time. And I just want to know what should I do?'

'Well, there we are, doc,' said Grav, 'that's Mrs Jones' problem. What's the answer then?'

And the doctor said, 'Mrs Jones. Now then, firstly, don't worry. It's a very natural thing. I understand that you're worried, but you are very right, don't hit him, or do anything like that to him. But if I can just tell you, it's just a matter of experience, of growing up. He's finding new experiences; he's finding things out about himself, so there's no need for you to worry at all.'

And Grav, live on air on Radio Wales, said, 'Yes, there we are Mrs Jones. Very good advice from the doc there. And if it's of any comfort to you, I'm still doing it!'

My God, he was a huge loss, wasn't he?

Nic Parry

I'm going back nearly 25 years. It was a very exciting time in the world of broadcasting in Wales. S4C was in its infancy, and I was asked to commentate on a wrestling series, no less. As can be imagined, the interest beforehand was enormous, and one of the main reasons for this was the announcement that the giant of a Welshman, the Lion, Ray Gravell, was going to be presenting it.

What has stayed with me more than anything is his kindness. I remember once addressing him as our 'Caradog Caredig' (Kind Caradog). As a huge fan of Dafydd Iwan, he knew exactly who 'Caradog y Cawr' (Caradog the Giant) was, and he loved the title I bestowed on him. But there were grounds for me to christen him like this, and I remember three examples of his tender care and his kindness towards me.

We were on the verge of our first ever broadcast of *Reslo*. Everyone was so nervous and anxious. Ray, as usual, was a bundle of excitement, asking if he looked OK, sounded OK, was saying the right things. Suddenly, it was time to give the first commentary on a brand-new sport.

As I raised the mike to my lips, I felt this strong hand on my shoulder, and these words being whispered in my ear. 'Remember Nic, nobody knows more about wrestling than you.' A complete lie of course, but the words of a man who in his own nervous state had obviously noticed that I was also very nervous, and he wanted to help and support me. The commentary, as a result, was so much more confident.

One of the most popular and amusing aspect of the series was listening to the referees, very often Irish, doing their very best to count from one to ten in Welsh. It was a huge worry for them. In fact, it was torturous and caused huge trauma before the combat even began. Within minutes to the start of one broadcast, Ray was missing. Everybody was ready, but no presenter, and everyone rushed around looking for him. Where was he? He was bent over in a dark, dusty corner at the back of the stage, giving two of the referees a last-minute lesson in counting in Welsh. He didn't see me, but I heard him encouraging and praising even when 'pump' (five) came out as pwmp instead of *pimp*, and he did his encouraging full of his characteristic enthusiasm. The referees had huge smiles on their faces, and went into the ring happily confident, and that was because a humble giant gave his time to help them.

But, the best example perhaps of his care, which was enveloped in sensitiveness, was the time when I was asked, as one of the commentary team, to let the wrestlers put us in a couple of holds. These fighters were huge men, and very often quite rough. One of the holds on the menu was to turn us on our faces, push our legs up our backs and pull our arms back to form the shape of a crab. Ray went first, and when he got up he said straight away, 'I'll do Nic.' And he did, with a care that was so tender, but he didn't reveal that to the others who were watching.

He must have seen something in my eyes as I was watching the others. He didn't say a word, only that he would do me. There wasn't a suggestion of humiliating or belittling me, he just wanted to look out for me.

I'll never forget his company, his zestful enjoyment and fun, but above everything his caring generosity and kindness.

Eleri Siôn

I was at college when I met Grav for the first time. I had started working in the BBC Cymru Sports Department on Saturdays in my final year, and our paths crossed. As a supporter, meeting any ex-international players would be a bit of an occasion, but meeting Grav was on another level because he was also a television star, and had secured his place as an established broadcaster. The thing that made him so special was that he made me feel that I, even when I was only working on Saturdays for Radio Cymru, was the giant in the broadcasting world and not HIM!

He always had the time and patience to give his attention to everyone. He had the natural ability to make every person feel that they were special. I felt a lot taller after being in his company. He would always have words of encouragement and support, and then the question, 'How's my voice?' followed by a mischievous smile.

I remember seeing Mari at Carmarthen's Morrisons. We were on our way to the west, and she invited Dave, my husband, and I to call and see them. So that's what we did. This was the time when Ray had his prosthetic leg. The first thing he did was pull off his leg to show us the Scarlets badge which had been printed on it. And then he showed us the watch he had received from the Scarlets. On the watch there was a personal message for him. He read the message in disbelief and also so full of emotion. He couldn't believe that they thought so highly of him. He was a giant of a man, but there wasn't an ounce of self-importance about him.

One of my favourite Grav stories was the one when he smashed one of the South African players on a Lions tour. The referee called him over and reprimanded him for the tackle being dangerously late, and Grav answered, 'Sorry, ref, I got there as soon as I could!'

Dot Davies

The first time I met Grav was in Australia on the 2001 Lions tour. Grav was in the middle, with around 40 supporters surrounding him, supporters from Wales, from England, from Ireland and Scotland. Everybody laughing themselves silly. Then Grav decided to be the conductor, and the singing started: 'Sosban Fach', 'Calon Lân', 'The Fields of Athenry', 'Flower of Scotland'. And then the joke came. Yes, he didn't have enough voice left to sing 'Swing Low'. But you know what, that was the thing about Grav. The English fans loved him even more after that. He had a way, didn't he? It didn't matter; he was just a natural leader.

I got to know him properly through working in the Sports Department of BBC Radio Cymru mainly. I was an innocent little researcher, and this giant would walk into the department, and he was a giant! Nobody could make me blush like Grav, and once he realised this, well, he enjoyed doing it. He would open the department door, and it was a huge open-plan room, with around 60 staff working there, maybe more. He would come in and shout at the top of his voice, 'Dot, Dot, Dot!' Everybody would stop their work. They'd look at him first, then turn to look at me, and my face would be the same colour as the Scarlets shirt. And he'd laugh, and I would go redder and redder. But then I would say hello, and he'd give me a huge cwtsh.

Oh, how I miss seeing that door open, and even miss the teasing.

Producers

Geraint Rowlands

Well, the first thing to say about Grav is that he was never quiet! As someone who shared a room with him on many occasions, when we were away with rugby related work in foreign parts, it has to be said that he was so noisy. He would be noisy when he was awake, talking without stop and wanting my opinion and advice, asking if I was happy with his work and this, that and the other. Then, once he was asleep, he would snore. He was a loud snorer! I would wake up often to Grav asking things like, 'Ger, Ger, why are you sleeping in the bath?' and that's how it was when I shared a room with him.

We were broadcasting live rugby on S4C in the middle of the '90s and Grav was integral to everything. He would do the interviews at the side of the pitch with players and coaches. There was nobody to touch him doing this sort of work, because he knew everybody. He knew how the players would react in different situations. They genuinely trusted him. This obviously secured the best content for our viewers. But then, over the talk-back – the system we had to keep in touch with me as I produced and directed the game – he would always, after doing every interview during the match which was still going on of course, get on the talk-back and ask, 'Ger, Ger, were you happy with that?' Of course I would be happy with his interview, but there would be a multitude of things happening and all of them needing my attention. So in the end I would get fed up and tell him, 'Grav, Grav, radio silence'. Then there would be a pause, before I would hear his voice again saying, 'Ger, Ger!' 'Yes?' 'Over!' He enjoyed the term 'over', even in phone calls. He would phone me two or three times a day; again, just to check that I was happy with his work. At the end of our chats he would say, 'Ger, Ger... Over!' and off he'd go.

We were really good friends, and he would look after me on a few occasions. At a game where Cardiff were playing Newport, there was a South African coaching Newport, and he was quite a fiery character. His name was Ian McIntosh. He had also been South Africa's coach. Newport lost quite heavily to Cardiff at Cardiff Arms Park that day and McIntosh was blaming everybody, and the one who was most at fault was the S4C television producer, because we had overrun for some reason and the kick-off had to be delayed by five minutes. So, as far as Ian McIntosh was concerned, it was our fault that they had lost the game. Anyway, at the end of the game, Grav came on the talk-back, 'Ger, Ger, it's... it's Ian McIntosh... he wants to kill you!' And I can remember thinking, this doesn't sound good. 'Don't come out of the truck,' which is where we were directing the game's coverage. 'Don't come out of the truck until I say that it's safe for you to do so. Leave it to me!' And, of course, I would trust Grav in such circumstances. Then, after about ten minutes, Grav came back on the line again and said, 'Ger, Ger, it's safe for you to come out now.' By then he and Ian McIntosh were the best of friends, and he didn't want to half kill me, and everything was OK, thanks to Grav. That's the kind of guy he was. He would look after your back, so kind and generous, and that story tells you the kind of person he was.

He was hopeless with cars! I remember travelling late with him once from somewhere, landing at Bristol Airport, and then having to pick up a rental car late at night. Both of us couldn't work out where the handbrake was on this car. So I got out of the car, and went to look for someone who could help. Grav was in the passenger seat, and by some miracle he found the button for the handbrake, and felt it would be a good idea to push it. Well, of course, what happened then was, as he was sitting in the passenger's seat, the car started to roll backwards in the direction of other cars that were parked there. All I could hear behind me was, 'Ger, Ger, I've found it! I've found the handbrake button.' So, as to avoid smashing a car, I had to run, jump in, and put my foot on the brake just in time before it went into the other cars.

But, of course, in a situation such as this, he would be so keen to celebrate the fact that he had found the button (and the fact that he was going home to Mynydd-y-Garreg) that he would not be aware of what was happening around him. He would be the same on every trip, wherever we would land, at Bristol or Cardiff airports, he would be the first on the M4 returning west and home to Mynydd-y-Garreg and to Mari, Manon and Gwenan. That was his mountain. That's where his rock was, and that's where his heart was.

I remember when my father, Dafydd Rowlands, was the archdruid and they were looking for someone to take over the 'Ceidwad y Cledd' (Sword Bearer) duties. I remember him asking me, 'What do you think? Would Grav be interested in doing it?' Rather than giving him my answer, I put the two in contact with each other – they knew each other already. Grav came over to the house, and they shared a bottle of red wine, a Shiraz from Australia, that became a bit of a favourite with Grav from then on. Of course, Grav felt it would be an honour, but also a duty for him to accept the appointment. And I can remember later that he even travelled back from South Africa, where he was commentating on the Lions tour, to be part of the Bridgend National Eisteddfod announcement ceremony.

In the procession Dad was walking just behind Grav through the streets. Of course, everyone would recognise Grav, and were reacting as they would see him. Someone shouted from the crowd, 'Grav, Grav, why aren't you in South Africa?' Grav answered gracefully, with the Sword in his hand, 'This is far more important than that!' That underlined the importance of the position to him, and all the prestige and honour he felt as he carried the Sword. Years later, of course, he had the honour of transferring the duties to Robin McBryde, and I know that that was very important to him.

I remember Dad telling me that he had discussed Grav's appointment with Hywel Teifi Edwards. Hywel Teifi had come to the conclusion that working on the lines for the electricity board was the reason that there was so much life, energy and power in Grav, and that he was, in fact, full of electricity! Hywel Teifi then came out with the immortal words, 'Yffach, is this a person you could trust with a sword in his hand?' They had a lot of fun discussing the matter.

We went away as families once. Mari, my wife and the girls had travelled up to Stratford in the afternoon, because there was a game on Saturday evening. Grav and I had been to Dublin and, as a treat, what I did was to arrange a bottle of wine for him for the journey up to Stratford. Of course, I couldn't have a drop as I was driving, but Grav could have a glass now and again. We got stuck in traffic on the M5, and it was very bad. Nothing had moved for a quarter of an hour. Grav decided that he wanted a chat with the people in the car next to ours. So out of the car he goes, with a glass of red wine in his hand – I was in the fast lane, remember! And there he was, talking with everyone in their cars, with the glass of red wine raised in the air dramatizing every story. There was no problem with this at all, until the traffic started to move! I had no idea where he had disappeared to, and of course I had to start moving, in the fast lane, in the middle of all the traffic, because everybody else was moving along. In the end he arrived from somewhere, full of concern and panic. 'Jesus Ger, I thought you were going to go without me.' Yes, he wanted to see Mari, Manon and Gwenan, as always.

Keith Davies (Keith Bach)

Right, how did I get to know Grav, first. Obviously, I had seen him play at Stradey Park, having been going there since I was about four or five years old with my father. But the first time I actually spoke to Grav was when my parents were having a new bathroom in the house, and they had gone to a company called Sharpe & Fisher. Without them knowing it, who was working for them at the time was Ray. He didn't stay long in the job, a year or two I think, and he had never sold a bathroom suite until my family bought one there. Anyway, he was the salesman who persuaded Mum and Dad to go for this bargain of a bathroom suite. Well, it was the ugliest one I have ever seen in my life to be honest. Until the day we left the house, this was the bathroom suite, some ugly dark chocolate colour, quite disgusting really. My father had tried to get rid of it many times, but Mum would always refuse, saying, 'No, Grav sold it to us!'

My father ran a training centre for adults with special educational needs. Dad was a guy who loved his sports. He was a huge fan of the Swans and the Scarlets. Every summer, at the training centre, they would have a sports day and they would always have someone famous to open the event, top celebrities. My father would note how they would arrive, do their speech, open the event, and then stay for about half an hour to socialise and accept praise and thank-yous before leaving. Fair play to them all for coming, and doing what was asked of them. Well, one year Grav was invited. He came, did his speech, and opened the sports day, but then he stayed all day. When Dad looked in the car park at the end of the day, he saw that Grav's car was still there. So he asked someone, 'Has Grav had a lift home then? His car is still here.' No, Grav was out on the field, helping to clear all the equipment that had been used during the day.

My father was extremely ill for a period of time at Llanelli hospital. By that time I had met Grav many times, but I didn't know him really well. He had come in to visit his Aunty Babs, who happened to be in the hospital at the same time as my father. I happened to bump into him in the corridor, and he asked, 'Hey, what are you doing here?' I explained that my father was extremely ill, and he went to see him that night and had a chat with him. He went to see him again the following night on his way to see Aunty Babs. Grav then asked me,

'Are you going somewhere this summer then?'

I answered, 'No, we had planned to take the kids to France. But no, we're not going now because of Dad's illness.' He was getting better, but still not right.

And Grav said, 'Hey, I had a word with your father about this last night. He was saying that you had promised to take the kids. Listen, if you have promised the children, and promised your dad that you'll go... you're going.'

And I answered, 'Noooo, we can't. We can't go Grav and leave Dad. Nobody will go to see him.'

'I'll go to see him,' said Grav.

In the end, between my father and Grav, we were persuaded to go on our holidays, and came back to find that Grav had been going to see my father twice a day, every day, when we were away!

When I first worked with Grav at the BBC, Grav would obviously create a lot of noise. But he could get people to do things that nobody else could dream of getting them to do. He came into Radio Cymru, and he was looking for CDs for his programme with Frank Hennessy on Radio Wales. If I or somebody else would be looking for a CD, we would be on our knees searching the lower shelves or on a chair searching the top shelves. But Grav? No. All he'd do was turn to the girls and greet them, 'Girls, girls, how are you this morning, you're beautiful. Oh, you look lovely this morning... Do any of you know where this CD I'm looking for is?' And of course they would get up and look for it for Grav. He wouldn't have to do a thing.

On one of those days, a hot day, he was wearing his Rockport short-sleeved shirt and Chino trousers. He tipped a glass of water over his Chinos in a rather unfortunate area, which left a very obvious wet patch. What he did, of course, was take his trousers off in the office, and put them on the radiator to dry. There he was, in his boxer shorts, greeting every guest as they came in as if it was an everyday occurrence.

During the same period the Lions were playing Argentina, if I remember rightly, in Cardiff. 'Listen,' he said, 'the traffic will be terrible today you know. There's no chance of getting a lift in is there? If I came to your house, would you give me a lift in?'

'Of course,' I said, without realising that the traffic would be as bad for me as it would have been for him. But, there we are, he was Grav. We'd do these things for him.

The kids were quite small then, the eldest about 11, 12, and I had told them, 'Hey, Grav is calling round tonight boys. Grav is coming tonight.' Anyway, around half past five there was a knock on the door. Well, a knock and walk in. He wouldn't wait for someone to answer the door as he shouted, 'The eagle has landed!' But who was also with him and wanting a lift was Garan Evans, the Scarlets' wing, and the kids were HUGE Scarlets fans. Of course, the kids ran down the stairs towards Grav, and he held out his arms; but they ran straight past him towards Garan Evans to ask him for his autograph! They took no notice of Grav, not realising who he was to be honest. Grav just turned and looked, 'Hey, that's the last time I'm coming here!'

As far as broadcasting was concerned there was never a dull moment, as you can imagine. We would sometimes have huge fall-outs! I remember broadcasting live from Trinity College, Carmarthen, for his radio programme from south-west Wales. Something had happened during the programme – I can't remember what – but as we were walking back to our cars we were shouting at each other

until we were blue in the face, blaming each other for what had happened. Anyway, we got into our cars and drove off. The next thing, my mobile went...

'Yes Grav, what do you want?'

'We're friends now, aren't we?'

'Yes Grav, we're friends.'

'Pull into the next lay-by then.'

After stopping at the next lay-by, Grav came out of his car, and I got out of mine. Grav gave me this huge hug, 'Friends, yes friends!'

We had to do the *Grav o'r Gorllewin* (Grav from the West) programme very cheaply. I don't think anyone was ever paid to be on the programme. Once we said it was for Grav's programme, everyone agreed, including the ones who would come to sing live in the studio, people like Brigyn, Meinir Gwilym and Fflur Dafydd. They all came to sing without receiving a penny, and were doing so because it was Grav.

If a guest would pull out or cancel on the morning of the broadcast, Grav would pick up the phone and would call one of two people, either Clive Rowlands or Hywel Teifi. Hywel's initial response would be,

'Oh, Gravell! What the hell do you want this morning again?'

'Respected, Venerable, Doctor, Professor. Would you be willing to consider coming on the programme this morning?'

'To talk about what, Gravell?'

That morning, as it happened, the theme was the hair fashion of the 1960s! And honestly Grav, somehow, persuaded Professor Hywel Teifi Edwards to discuss the hair fashion of the 1960s.

And talking of Clive Rowlands, Clive was one of our regular listeners, him and his wife Margaret. Grav would mention them often, and he always referred to them as 'Lord and Lady of Cwmtwrch'. We broadcasted live from Cwmtwrch once, and when we arrived the first person he was hoping to see at Cwmtwrch hall was Clive Rowlands. But there was no sign of Clive or his wife. As the show went on – it was a two-hour show – about a quarter of an hour before the end, and Grav having been so worried the whole time as to where Clive was, worrying that he had upset him in some way...

'I haven't said anything to upset Clive, have I?'

'No Grav, you haven't said anything to upset Clive.'

'Are you sure? I was speaking with him last week, you see, and everything was OK. I haven't done anything, have I?'

'No Grav, everything's fine.'

And then, with a quarter of an hour left of the programme, who walked in but Clive and Margaret and, of course, live on air.

'Oh, here they are. They've arrived, Lord and Lady Cwmtwrch!'

And he went straight to Clive.

'Clive, come here for a chat before the show comes to an end.'

And, of course, Clive went to have a chat with Grav, and he introduced Clive.

'For all of you who don't know, Clive Rowlands is the only person to have played for, captained and coached, been a selector and a president of the Welsh Rugby Union, that's who he is! And do you know, what's more important than anything? Clive Rowlands was the man who selected me for my first cap!'

And Clive answered straight back. 'And remember, I was the one who dropped you too!'

'Well, on we go to the next song then, yes bois?' said Grav.

After every show, usually done at the Swansea studios, I would drive back to the office at the studios in Cardiff. Within around ten minutes of arriving, the phone would ring.

'Hey Keith Bach, Keith Baaaaach! Listen, was I good today?'

'Yes Grav, you were all right.'

'I was only all right?'

'No Grav, you were great!'

'Are you sure?'

'Yes, yes Grav, you were great, fantastic.'

'You're being honest with me now?'

'Yes Grav, you were great.'

'How do I know you're telling the truth?'

Usually, that's when I would put the phone down. But then, the phone would ring again in about ten minutes.

'Keith Bach, Keith Bach. Are you busy?'

'Um, no, not especially Grav.'

'OK, I'll phone you back when you're busy then.' And he'd put the phone down.

When we went to Glynneath, the village where Max Boyce was born, we were broadcasting using this small piece of kit which was no more than a phone. Again, it was very cheap. The best thing about it was that you could take it with you anywhere as long as there was a phone line. We also had to put an aerial up quite high to get a signal. So, we were in a café in Glynneath. Not only is the valley very narrow, and the hills around very high, some of the buildings on the main street are three storeys high, therefore hindering a signal. We were supposed to start at 8.30am, but with 25 minutes to go before the start of the programme, we still didn't have a signal. A co-worker of ours, Tomos Morse, went to sort it out as Grav was arriving.

'Right then boys, are we ready to go, are we ready to go?!'

'Not yet, Grav.'

'Where's Tomos?'

'Oh, Tomos is sorting a signal for the Comrex, that piece of kit I mentioned, so we can broadcast.'

'Where is he, where is he?'

And on that note, Grav looked up three floors and saw Tomos Morse leaning out of the highest window of this three-floor building, both hands holding the aerial, and his legs just about stuck inside the building to stop him from falling. Safe to say, we were breaking every health and safety rule and, on reflection, what he was doing was rather foolish.

Suddenly, Grav shouted, 'Tomos bach, what are you doing?' and a voice from above answered,

'I have to get this aerial right.'

Grav answered, 'Tomos, no, no, no, don't. Come back, come down, Tomos bach. It's not safe. You could fall and kill yourself...'

The voice from above answered again, 'Grav, if I can't get this signal sorted, you won't be going on air.'

'Well, carry on then Morse bach. Carry on!'

There's another story about this tiny little machine, the Comrex. I think we were in the small village of Llansaint, in the hall there, but there was no phone line. So, Tomos

Morse had to run a cable across the hall, through the car park, over the road, through this small field into a farmhouse where they had said they would be perfectly happy for us to use their phone line. When outside broadcasts like this happened, there would always be someone back in the studio in Cardiff playing the music. So Grav would say something like, 'And next we're going to hear Fflur Dafydd singing "Helsinki",' and then whoever was in Cardiff would play the song into the programme. As it happened, this time it was me who was in Cardiff, while the others were with Grav in Llansaint. As Grav was talking to one of the local guests, suddenly everything went dead. As we do, I waited about five seconds, then raised the volume of my fader and said, 'Unfortunately, we seem to have lost connection with Grav due to technical issues. We will be back with you as soon as possible,' and played some music. I tried to phone Grav then.

'Grav, Grav, what's wrong, what's happened?'

'Listen, the phone line we set up, it was going across the road you see.'

'Yes?'

'But this tractor came and went over it, and broke the line.'

Right, I played two or three more songs. Suddenly, the phone went. 'We're back, we're back! Put us back on air,' and I said, 'Well, thank you very much. Now we can go back to Ray Gravell in Llansaint.' Up with the fader again to put Grav back on air, and he went on to introduce the next song. As the song started my phone rang again. It was Grav. 'Listen, listen. The bloody tractor is on its way back!'

*

People would send CDs for us to play. We received a new CD from Gwyneth Glyn, *Wyneb Dros Dro*, and I told Grav,

'Listen. Play "Adra" (home), OK?'

'Oh right, yes. OK.'

'It's a fantastic song. You'll love it, Ray.'

'OK... well next, from Gwyneth Glyn's new CD, here's the song "Adra".'

Of course it starts in English, 'There is a town in North Ontario'. Before the song reached the words 'North Ontario', Grav had pressed stop. He looked at me and said, 'I'm not playing that.' He opened the fader and said, 'Apologies to you listeners at home. I don't play English songs on my programme. Huge apologies. Here's Meic Stevens and "Brawd Houdini".' I then said to him,

'Grav, trust me will you? Play that song. You'll love it.'

'No, I won't play English songs, no way!'

'Grav, just play the song will you?!'

In the end we persuaded him to play the song, 'There is a town in North Ontario' ... 'does unman yn debyg i gartre' (there's nowhere like home). By the end of the song Grav was amazed, and fell completely in love with it, and the tears were flowing down his cheeks. And, of course, Gwyneth Glyn sang the song live at his funeral in Stradey Park.

Another story. Grav came in to record with us on Radio Cymru some afternoons while Owen Money was live on air for Radio Wales. Grav came in to record, and went into Owen Money's studio. 'Hi Owen, all right?' (Owen was live on air, remember!). Owen sort of looked at him and said, 'Well, you listeners back home… um Ray Gravell has walked into the studio by here… yes Ray, we're live on air,' just so that he didn't swear. 'We're live on air Ray, so yes, do you want to say hello to…?'

'Well, hello, hello. What are you doing by here then, Owen?'

'Well, we're live on air Grav.'

'No, you're not. I'm supposed to be recording in this studio now.'

'No, we're live on air Grav!'

'Well I am…'

'You're not supposed to be here, Grav.'

'Yes I am! I'm supposed to be recording in this studio!'

'Well…' Owen started laughing.

'Well, I better check, Owen!' and off he went out of the studio and Owen Money's programme was able to carry on. In about half an hour, all you could hear on the radio was Owen Money laughing uncontrollably. Grav had walked back into Owen's studio, and his programme was still going out live and he said, 'Owen! Right studio, but wrong day man!'

*

Grav was invited to be a guest speaker at the Trinity College Dublin ex-alumni annual dinner. People like Yeats, Seán O'Casey, Oscar Wilde and Jonathan Swift had been speakers at the dinner. Academics and philosophers too, as there was so much history to the college which was one of the most important universities in the world.

Grav was invited by his friend, former Ireland full back Dick Spring, to speak at the dinner. Until that day, no-one without a degree had ever been a guest speaker there, as all previous speakers had more than one degree and numerous letters after their names. Even Grav was nervous that day, according to him, when he arrived in the large hall of Trinity College Dublin. All the guests were in their academic robes, and he had left Carmarthen Grammar School at 15 and gone to work straight away with the electricity board.

Grav got up to his feet and thanked them for the welcome. There was a lot of looking around at each other, as if to say, 'What's this pleb doing here in our midst?' Dick Spring was a graduate of the university of course, and also, at the time, was Ireland's Minister of Foreign Affairs, and that's important to this story. Grav got to his feet and said, 'I'd like to thank Dick Spring for the invitation. It's such an honour, and I'm thinking of all the famous and illustrious people who've been in this position before me. I would really like to thank Dick, my great friend, who was a great full back for Ireland. On that note, I'm very glad that he's your country's Minister of Foreign Affairs, because if his rugby is anything to go by, he'd be a crap Minister of Defence!' And from that moment on, all the academics and pillars of high society at Trinity College Dublin were in his hands, and by the end of the speech they adored him.

When Dick Spring came over to Wales while he was still Ireland's Minister of Foreign Affairs, there was a lot of leg pulling and teasing. Dick Spring had arranged a Daimler to pick Grav up from the airport and take him to Trinity College Dublin when he went to speak there. So, just to pull his leg, Dick Spring said to Grav, 'Grav, I expect the same thing when I come to Cardiff.'

Radio Cymru were doing a series about cars at the time, and Grav had a word with Wyn Jones who was doing the programme. When Dick Spring landed at Cardiff Airport, the most beautiful Rolls Royce you ever saw was waiting for him. There were also two policemen on motorbikes to accompany him to his hotel in Cardiff.

A couple of years after we lost Grav, I was over in Dublin. There's a farmers' market, which not a lot of people know about, hidden in a car park behind offices not far from Temple Bar. I love going there. At one stall a woman would come from the west coast every Saturday to sell oysters. So, one morning, I went to the market and saw that this woman was there and I got talking to her.

'Oh, you're busy in the market here.'

'Oh yes, selling oysters.'

'Where do you come from?'

'Oh, we've come from the west coast. We drive down every

Saturday. Hey, that's a Welsh accent! Oh I love you Welsh,' she said. 'If it wasn't for a Welshman, we would've left our stall on our second day. I'm going back a few years now,' she said, 'and it was only our second Saturday trading at the Saturday Market in Dublin. I think he was an ex-Welsh rugby player. He had a red beard...'

'Was he called Ray Gravell?' I asked.

'Yes, yes, yes,' she said. 'He was lovely, the loveliest man I ever met!'

What had happened was that Grav had gone up to her and asked, 'Hey, how's trade today then?'

'Oh, not very good. We haven't sold a lot.'

'Give me the basket.'

And, as she said, the only thing she saw was Grav walking up the steps towards the High Street with a basket full of oysters, singing, 'In Dublin's Fair City, where the girls are so pretty... Cockles and mussels, alive, alive, oh!'

'And then,' she said, 'in about an hour's time he came back with loads of money and an empty basket. He'd sold them all at double the price we were asking for them.'

Every time someone introduced Grav as Ray Gravell who played for Llanelli, Wales, the Barbarians and the Lions, he would always say, 'Test Lion, Test Lion' and would then shout, 'and the Irish Wolfhounds!'

*

One final story says everything about Grav. When we were broadcasting in Swansea, every Friday we'd go from the BBC studios near the Glynn Vivian Art Gallery and go down this narrow alleyway behind the offices on the High Street, and there we'd have breakfast. It wasn't the most lavish of cafés, but it was run by an Irishman called Eamonn. Anyway, very often the call centre workers would be out having a cigarette when we walked down this alleyway, and Grav would always talk to everybody. There would also be two or three homeless people there too. One morning Grav, who would always give something to the homeless, noticed that there was a new guy there. We hadn't seen him before; he was quite young and he looked miserable. Grav went to his pocket and gave him £5 and said, 'You spend that on food now, you promise? You spend that on food!' 'Yea, yea,' said the guy, 'fine, fine.'

Anyway, I was down in Swansea doing something else in a week or two, and I was walking down the alleyway to have a cup of tea at the usual café. The young lad that Grav gave £5 to was there and he asked,

'Oh, is Grav with you?'

'Oh, no, he's not with us today, no, no.'

He went to his pocket and he had a receipt. 'Can you show him this?' He gave me the receipt just to show that he had bought sandwiches with Grav's money.

Everybody loved Grav.

Sion Thomas

I worked mostly with Grav as a producer/director at live rugby matches when he was at pitch side. He was like a people magnet.

I remember being out in Ireland. 'Sion, Sion, come to me now.' I looked down at the monitor in front of me and I can remember thinking, I recognise this guy that's with Grav, and I just had to go to him live. And Grav said to camera, 'Well, with me now is Christy Moore.' Waw, I thought, he's been able to get Christy Moore on our programme! Grav was brilliant. People had so much respect for him, and the fact that that respect and importance was reflected in our broadcast was amazing.

I remember another game in Ireland, a friendly between Wales and Ireland before a World Cup. Grav was out on the touchline and he had heard that they didn't have a copy of the Welsh National Anthem in Welsh. They had found a CD with 'Land of My Fathers' sung by some choir. But Grav was going berserk and was going around Lansdowne Road like a whirlwind. He was very upset, and was knocking on doors and came to the executive box of the president of the Irish Rugby Union. In he went, and demanded a word with the president. He told him that it was all an 'absolute disgrace!' In the end they found someone to sing 'Hen Wlad fy Nhadau'. Grav had saved the day once again.

But sometimes, and I'm sure that Grav wouldn't mind me saying this, he could be a bloody nuisance. We would be broadcasting rugby matches live and he was an integral part of the team. I would have to direct live, and there were some times when Grav would have to be quiet. There was a code between us which had been developed over the years. Grav would sometimes try to reach me when I was very busy trying to direct. I would have to tell him, 'No, not now Grav. Radio silence!' Then Grav would answer, 'Oh, yes, no problem, I understand Sion. I understand perfectly, over and OUT! OUT! OUT!' That's exactly what he'd say. There would have been less noise if I'd just spoken to him!

There was a game up in Scotland, a Six Nations match in Edinburgh, Scotland v Wales. Wales were playing very well and halfway to winning the Grand Slam for the first time in many years. Grav was there on the touchline. There was about ten minutes to go before we were on air, then five minutes and then 'two minutes to transmission' and we would have around half an hour of build-up, and it was quite a complicated programme. I looked down at the bank of monitors in front of me, and I could see that there was this scuffle going on on one of the cameras. I can remember thinking, blimey, what's going on down there? The next thing, Grav's voice came through. 'Sioni, Sioni! Come to me live, come to me live now.' I said to him, 'Grav, we are about to go on air. Radio silence.' I was expecting the 'OUT! OUT!' But, 'Sioni, Sioni! Come to me, come to me now,' came again. I looked closer, and I saw that Grav was holding someone in a headlock, and I thought, what the hell is going on here?

We went to the 'titles'. Gareth Roberts said, 'Welcome to

Murrayfield, and we're going straight down to the touchline to Ray Gravell.' There Grav was with this guy in a headlock. Who was he? The Scotland coach, Matt Williams, an Australian who coached Scotland for two or three years. A tall, good-looking guy with longish silvery hair – he didn't look like the typical coach. So down we went to Grav and Matt Williams in a headlock, and Grav's introduction was, 'Welcome, welcome. I've got Robert Redford here, half an hour before kick-off. Robert Redford, how do you think the game is going to go?' And Matt Williams was laughing and thought it was hilarious. He had a game in half an hour, and Grav had broken every protocol.

When you think of the Scottish Rugby Union, they are the most conservative union and the most anti-media from the standpoint of giving permission to interview players or coaches during a game. They were off-limits. The fact that Ray had the Scotland coach in a headlock at the top of our programme was a huge scoop for us. The BBC were furious, because they didn't get permission for any interviews, and the fact that S4C had succeeded to interview the Scotland coach live, half an hour before kick-off, was infuriating for them. The Scotland press officer came over and was hammering the door of our truck like a banshee, shouting all kinds of complaints! But, there we are, that's how Grav was. Nothing came of the complaints, and S4C had a scoop, thanks to Grav.

On a personal note, he would phone me time and time again during the rugby season, sometimes around ten times a day. 'Any news? Any news?' and to talk about anything and everything. On the day before he died so suddenly out in Spain, I was up in Newcastle in a meeting, and just before going into the meeting Grav called on the phone. I nearly ignored it thinking I'd call him back, but I answered and we had a lovely chat. He was out in Spain with the girls, enjoying of course, and the next day we heard the news that we had lost him. I am so glad that I answered that call, and had that last conversation with him. It's so difficult to believe that he has been gone for over ten years now.

It was a special experience for me to direct his funeral live on television. I had expected there to be a crowd, and for it to be emotional, but blimey, the whole of Wales was in mourning. I was so grateful for the opportunity, and it was nice to be able to do something for the old friend, in paying his final tribute.

It was fun travelling with him wherever we went: Ireland, Australia, wherever. Everybody knew Grav. But he hated being away too long. When travelling with him, once the game was over, all he wanted to know was what were the arrangements for getting home, because he couldn't wait to go home to Mari and the girls. He wouldn't like to be too far from home. But it was a great experience to work with him. He was unique, and everybody wanted to and were glad to speak to him.

Marc Griffiths (Marci G)

Well, I had the opportunity to work with Grav a few years back by now, on the show *Grav o'r Gorllewin* (Grav from the West) on Radio Cymru. He was presenting a two-hour programme from 8.30 to 10.30 in the mornings. My job was to make sure that everything was ready in the studio, that all the songs were ready to play and, of course, that the coffee or tea was ready for him. I can remember that he didn't want milk or sugar in his coffee or tea. Yes, that was my job, and it was an experience, unforgettable to be honest, because he was such a character.

During the programme we would interview people and Grav, of course, would talk to everybody. He could reach all kinds of people, young or old. What was great about Grav was that he would introduce himself to everyone he would meet, even though there was no need to because everybody recognised him. But this is what he would do, and it's proof of how humble he was as a person. I travelled with him across the west of Wales, and had the pleasure of meeting his biggest fans. I must admit, he would trip over cables, push the wrong buttons, and the words that followed would be, 'Wps y deri dando'.

When the songs would be playing on his programme Ray would be on the phone with friends, or phoning the betting shop in Crosshands to put a little bet on some horse or other. After the show we would call in on the way home at Rhiannon's Café in Crosshands to have a breakfast. Everybody would know him at the café, and we would be

there for an hour or two talking away. On his birthday I remember giving him a picture of Owain Glyndŵr's Senedd as a present. The emotion on his face was proof of how much his hero meant to him.

Dewi Wyn Williams (Dewi Chips)

In 1992 Ray had a role in the film *Damage* directed by Louis Malle, with Jeremy Irons, Juliette Binoche and Miranda Richardson among some of the stars involved.

I was working as a script editor for the BBC at the time, and Ray was a rugby commentator. I had come to know Ray through my father, the actor Glyn Pensarn, who was friends with Dafydd Hywel, one of Ray's best friends. We both would have short chats with a bit of leg-pulling in the corridors.

Ray was so excited to be in this film with the role of Dr Fleming's chauffer. And, consistent with his obsessive nature, he was very nervous, even though he only had one line which was, 'To the station, sir?' And because I knew him and worked in the drama department, Ray would like to rehearse his line as he passed me in the corridor.

'Oh, Dew bach, Dew bach. How would *you* say this line?' before stopping dramatically, spreading his arms out wide and reciting the line, 'To the station, sir?'

And, of course, I would correct him or tease him some more!

'No Ray. You're accenting the wrong word.'

'Wrong word? Wrong word?! Whoa! Please tell me, Dew bach. How do I do it properly then?' And I would then, of course, give him different permutations every time, for weeks. Permutations like, '*To* the station, sir? or 'To *the* station, sir? or 'To the station, *sir?*' sending Ray into a flat spin.

'Whoa! Don't. Don't Dew bach. You're completely confusing me now!' And he would walk away down the corridor reciting at the top of his voice, 'To the station, sir?' in all the different ways.

I was so pleased to see that the line appeared in the film, and had avoided the cutting-room floor. The accent must have been on the right word by Ray, and his hero Louis Malle must have been pleased.

Actors and Correspondents

Gary Slaymaker

The first time I came across Grav was when I was a clerk at the Recorded Programmes Library at the end of the '80s. I was, at the time, marketing the programme *Street Life*. I went in one morning to collect some tapes from the BBC Radio Wales shelves, and I happened to overhear a chat between Grav and a doctor on his weekly programme. That morning they were discussing 'nocturnal emissions', and the doctor was talking about young men having wild dreams which turned into wet dreams.

The doctor said, 'It can be quite traumatic!'

And Grav said, 'Yes, I understand that. One minute you're asleep, and the next you're awake and you're covered in the stuff!'

Oh yes, he did say that. The producer's head was on the table as he was pounding it with his fist, and everybody else was laughing until they were weak at the knees.

By the early '90s I was working regularly for BBC Swansea, and I would bump into Grav at least once a week.

As far as I can remember, Grav is the only one to sneak up behind me and get a hold of me to tickle me, and call me 'Slei Bach' (Little Sly). There's nothing small about me, is there now?!

During that time, when I would regularly see him, he came up to me one morning and said,

'Slei, Slei, you know your films, don't you?'

'Well, yes Grav...'

'Have you heard of Louis Malle?'

'Yes, he's one of the most famous film directors,' I said, and started reeling off all the films that he had directed. And I asked him, 'Why do you ask, Grav?'

'Well, I've just had a part in a film he's making. Do you think I'll do all right?'

'Well, you'll be great,' I said. 'You'll be fine. This guy is great with his actors, so listen to everything he says to you.'

Damage was the name of the film that Grav appeared in. Even though it wasn't a big part, it was an important one as he was Jeremy Irons' chauffer.

Around six months later he was back, and oh, he had enjoyed himself, and was full of praise for Louis Malle and also for Jeremy Irons and Juliette Binoche. I saw the film about a year later and I can remember him coming up to me and asking,

'Was I OK, was I all right?'

'Grav man, considering the company you were keeping, you were marvellous!'

And that's how Grav was: talented and brave on the rugby

field, but talented off the field as well. But then again, he was so shy and humble; it was difficult sometimes to understand why he would talk with you the way he did.

Around six months later there was a drama on BBC1 called *Filipina Dreamgirls*. Grav was one of the characters and, if truth be told, the only reason I carried on watching the whole film was to see Grav's performance in it. He was playing a character who worked for the council as a rat catcher, and someone who'd just lost his mother and had gone out to the Philippines to look for a partner. From all the characters and stories within the film, it was Grav's part that captured the audience's imagination. Once again, I bumped into Grav on the Tuesday after the film had been on, and I told him how much I had really enjoyed his part in the film. Grav, again, was amazed that I thought he had done such a good job.

Grav and Frank Hennessy did a 'Noson Lawen' community concert/evening for Radio Wales. They would go to different towns and villages throughout Wales for a night of entertainment, using local talent. I can remember Radio Wales contacting me to ask if I would do a 'stand-up' at one of these evenings at the Black Lion in Lampeter. One thing they did say to me was that I had to be politically correct, and my jokes had to be clean. Anyone who has seen my stand-up routine would know that these words pay no relation to my set. So I was a little bit nervous, because I had to write a new set, completely clean and, to top it all, I was in front of my home crowd, people whom I'd known since

I was a little boy. I did my set, and I still felt a bit twitchy when Grav came up and just said,

'I know it's difficult. He's performing in front of friends and family.' On top of that he paid tribute to my father, because my father had played a lot of rugby and had done a lot in the rugby environment after playing. Grav knew him.

Completely uncalled for again, but just shows the kind of man he was. He wanted to thank me from the bottom of his heart for my work. Like so many others, I can only think of good things to say about Grav.

Dafydd Hywel

It was interesting how I first met Grav. I'm going back to the early '70s now. I was playing for Cymry Caerdydd RFC against Llanelli Athletic, and Llanelli were playing at Stradey Park that afternoon. I can't remember who they were playing, but Carwyn James was there. *Miri Mawr* (a very popular children's TV series in Welsh) was at the peak of its popularity at the time. And that is how I was introduced to Grav for the first time.

'Do you know this chap, Raymond?' Carwyn asked. Grav had no idea who I was. 'Here's Caleb' (one of the characters in the series), he said. And I was Caleb to Grav from that moment on and we became the best of friends.

I did about four films with him I think. I remember one of them we did, *Rebecca's Daughters*. We had a lot of fun doing it with Peter O'Toole. Marina Monios, the make-up lady, told me this story.

Grav was in his costume, dressed as Rebecca (so in a lady's costume), and he had seen O'Toole going into the caravan to have his make-up done. So Marina told the story that Grav came in and Marina said,

'Oh Peter, this is Ray.' He didn't show a lot of interest, only a 'Oh, how are you?'

But the two got talking, and Ray said,

'Oh, I'm friendly with a friend of yours, Richard Harris.'

'Oh yes, I know Richard Harris. How do you know Richard?'

'He's good friends with Terry James, the musician. That's how I met him.'

And Marina said, 'Oh, Peter, Ray used to play rugby.'

'Oh yes?' O'Toole loved his rugby. 'Who did you play for?'

'Oh, Llanelli,' said Grav.

O'Toole started to show some interest in Grav.

'*&§$ Llanelli?' There were a lot of 'fs' in Peter O'Toole's vocabulary.

'Yes,' said Grav.

'When was that then?'

'Oh, a few years ago now.'

'How many times did you play for them then?'

'Nearly 500 times,' said Grav.

'*&§$ hell, hang on now!' and he was starting to get really excited.

'So you know Phil Bennett and Gareth Edwards and all those boys?'

'Oh yes,' said Grav.

'You played against them, did you?'

'I played against them and with them.'

'You played with them and against them. *&§$ hell, hang on now, what position were you playing then?'

'Oh, centre.'

'Oh, who was the best player you played against then?'

And Grav answered, 'Mike Gibson of Ireland.'

And suddenly, this Laurence of Arabia got up to his feet, flung the towel that was around his shoulders, and said,

'Are you telling me that... You're not **THE RAY GRAVELL** are you?'

And Grav said, 'Yes I am.'

'Well *&§$ hell! Wait 'til I go back to London and tell the boys that I'm making a film with Ray Gravell!'

I also remember us filming in Caerphilly Castle. I was acting this 'header'; I was the 'mountain fighter'. I said to Karl Francis, the director (we were in the castle itself, so the views were fantastic), that we were supposed to win this fight. So I suggested,

'I tell you what, Karl. I'll go over to Grav, and tell him to finish the fight off.'

'Good idea DH, good idea,' he said.

So I went up to Grav and told him, 'Listen now, just before I finish this bloody fight, I will look at you, right? And I'll be pointing; then you come in.' Well, bloody hell, he came in; I

thought Grav was going to kill him! Oh, we had a lot of fun doing that film.

We did a lot of 'nosweithe joio' (fun nights/concerts) together – Grav, myself, Sue Roderick, and Goss (Euron Davies) on the piano. Ray would tell his stories, and people would be in stitches as he recalled these stories.

He knew so many people, and would love to chat over a pint or a little whiskey. It was Grav who introduced me to

Jack Daniels whiskey. I was playing Jac Daniels in *Pobol y Cwm* at the time, around 1984, and Grav bought a bottle for me. 'This will be nice for you,' he said with a huge laugh.

Emyr Wyn

I knew Grav of course for many years – since the '70s. He was a fan of our group Mynediad am Ddim and we came across each other a lot because he played for the Scarlets. But, I think the first time I actually worked with him was on a programme called *Teulu-ffôn* on S4C. It was a live broadcast, on a Thursday night if I remember correctly, and there were three of us presenting. Because it was going out live, we had to do a little (well, quite a bit of) practice and preparation. All day Wednesday we would prepare for the Thursday, and go 'on air' at 7.30, or 8pm or whatever the time was, for half an hour. It was a quick and busy programme to do. People would phone in to take part in competitions and activities, so we had to have some sort of order. But Grav was never one for order or procedure. He enjoyed doing things 'off the cuff' and it was one of his main strengths of course. So, I was in the middle as a kind of 'anchorman', very often trying to keep him under control. But it was so, so important to have the practice on the Wednesday to prepare everything, so that everyone knew what to do. We would be in the studio on Thursday morning having three or four run-throughs before doing the actual programme that night.

Therefore, every Wednesday, we would all be at the HTV studios having a practice and a run-through. I remember one Wednesday, turning up, Margaret Pritchard, myself, Gareth Roberts and Paul Jones the producer and director. We waited and waited, 5pm came and went, 6pm – we would work quite late on the Wednesdays. No sign of Grav. It was before the time of mobile phones, and nobody knew where he was. We did the rehearsing without him, and that was that. Then came Thursday morning, and who was the first in but Grav.

'Oooo, ooo, sorry boys, sorry boys. Ohhh, couldn't possibly make it yesterday afternoon or last night. I was so ill, I was sick in bed.'

'But you're better now?'

'Ooo, a lot better, a lot better, so so sorry.'

Then Paul Jones just turned around and asked him, 'Where were you really?'

'I was in bed, I was… I couldn't move!'

'Well, you were moving quite well on the Gnoll last night when Llanelli were playing Neath!'

Well, talk of laughing! It was quite serious also, as this was the time when his rugby was starting to become an obstacle to his new career. He would have to make a choice.

But he was so 'genuine' and so innocent in thinking that nobody would notice that he was playing for the Scarlets when he should have been working in Cardiff! I knew that Onllwyn Brace had threatened him on more than one occasion that he had to decide between rugby and his career in broadcasting. He had a final warning really. This was in the '84/85 season, and he stopped playing in '85. He played,

I believe, 485 times for the Scarlets, and he so wanted to reach the 500. There were only one or two players who had played 500 times for the Scarlets, and that was the reason he was so determined to reach that milestone. That's the reason, of course, why he lied. He just wanted to reach that goal, even though it was putting his new career in jeopardy. Yes, 'I was ill in bed, couldn't move.' I'll never forget Paul Jones' riposte, 'But you were moving very well for Llanelli

139

on the Gnoll last night.' And Grav answering, 'Ohhh, boys, ohooo, you've caught me now, you've caught me.'

I remember a rugby game being arranged on *Pobol y Cwm* when the two village teams, Cwmderi and Llanarthur, were playing each other. It was a special occasion, but I can't remember what, but I have a photo on the wall at home. Ray was playing for Cwmderi and Delme Thomas (Wales and Lions second row) was playing for Llanarthur. Ray thought the world of Delme, of course. This was going out in an episode of *Pobol y Cwm* around 1979–80. We played the game, but had to break it up for filming. Even in a game like this, Grav couldn't hold back. He would go at it 100 per cent, and thank God he was on our team! The game would be stopped to do some moves for filming, and then it was time to film a lineout. Dic Deryn and Dai (Sgaffalde) were in the lineout for Cwmderi, and Delme Thomas was in Llanarthur's lineout, and we were supposed to compete for the ball. The director came down from the scanner, 'Right, tell Emyr to let Delme win the ball.' We're talking here about one of the greatest lineout jumpers ever to play rugby, and he was jumping for Llanarthur against Dai Sgaffalde and bloody Dic Deryn for Cwmderi, with the director saying, 'Tell Emyr to let Delme win the ball!' And Delme turned around to us, and said with a little bit of a stutter, 'I... I'll try my best now, I... I... I'll try my best, boys.' Grav was in hysterics laughing. Just some wonderful memories, a lot of fun.

Rhys Bleddyn

I met Ray for the first time at the Barcud studios in Caernarfon, on a cold morning in the early '90s. We were performing monologs to be shown as part of an exhibition at the new Celitca Heritage Centre in Machynlleth – Ray was a Celtic warrior, and I a poet.

The studio looked enormous, with only one camera and an autocue, and even though Ray's personality filled the place, he was in a cold sweat and a bag of nerves.

'I can't do it. I don't know it! You'll have to have somebody else,' said Ray, standing next to the camera after cornering the director.

I shook hands with the worried giant, and offered, 'Would you like me to go over the lines with you in the green room?' I'll never forget his grateful smile.

Before we knew it, we were summoned back to the studio, and Ray was thanking me over and over again as we walked back there.

It was me to go first, and I don't think that helped to calm Ray's nerves. He was as white as a sheet, and he insisted that I stood next to the autocue, just in case he needed some help.

Of course, he was marvellous, and he hugged me at the end of his take, as if we were two real warriors having just conquered our enemy.

Three months later the situation was reversed. It was a scorching hot day in Llandaff, and it was my first day rehearsing *Pobol y Cwm*. I had been working in theatres for six years, but television was completely new to me. After a morning of inadequate read-throughs, it was lunchtime, and I had lost my co-actors in this enormous and unfamiliar place. I stood in the queue for lunch, feeling quite awkward and really uncomfortable in the midst of many familiar faces who were strangers to me. I hadn't talked to anyone as I paid; then I looked about trying to find somewhere quiet to sit on the periphery of all the celebrities and important people.

From the far corner I heard a loud roar, 'Rhys, come here, come here. It's Ray, here!' He had remembered my name even, let alone my face. He introduced me to everyone on his table.

Kindness was instinctive to Ray. He made me feel like a king in very unfamiliar surroundings, and I knew that I was in the company of a unique Welshman.

Gareth Roberts

The first time I came across him was at the old studios in Pontcanna, when we were doing a TV programme called *Teulu-ffôn*. It was a programme that went out live and was pioneering at the time, because people watching at home could phone in to compete in the competitions. Things like *Bwrw'r Sul*, or whatever, came later, but *Teulu-ffôn* was the first in the middle of the '80s. Emyr Wyn was the 'anchorman' and the other four presenters were Margaret Pritchard, who was doing continuity on HTV, Gaynor Davies, myself and Ray Gravell. And it was live wasn't it, and Ray had never done a live broadcast before, had he. So, you can all imagine... Even though people looked at Grav as a giant of a rugby legend, he was a nervous and insecure character in truth. He always needed to know, 'Was that OK?' or 'How's my voice today?' It was a habit. 'Gar, Gar, how's my voice today? ... Yee Ha, Yee Haaa!' like some cowboy!

But it was later, when we started to work on rugby broadcasts, that I got to know Grav properly and what came from that was, of course, a myriad of stories and anecdotes. At the first Welsh-language broadcast of a Wales international, he saw the *Grandstand* studio and took his chance. Grav was warned not to wear red, but his answer was, 'Wales are playing England in Cardiff in the Six Nations, and every Tom, Dick and Harry knows who I'm supporting!'

When Grav was doing touchline interviews at games some people would criticise him, saying that he wasn't always asking incisive questions, wouldn't ask difficult questions, but I never saw anyone refuse an interview with Grav. There is strict protocol as far as the rugby unions are concerned regarding interviews, and broadcasters must adhere to the rules and follow the procedures to interview people. Ray would see someone, like Sir Clive Woodward for example, and shout 'Clive' (because he'd been sharing a room with him on a Lions tour), and Clive would come over and we would get an interview there and then. He had that ability to persuade anyone to do an interview with him.

Another thing I also noticed about Grav, when we were

away at the Six Nations in Ireland, France, Scotland, England or Italy, was that he would do interviews with people on the street, and it struck and amazed me how he could remember people's names. He had an amazing memory for people's names, and he would be more than willing to give his time to people. He would draw people to him, wouldn't he; he was a second-to-none communicator. He would be equally at home with the likes of Joan Collins and Catherine Zeta-Jones or Will the butcher or whomever.

Grav loved going to Ireland, and he had many close friends there. 'What is an Irishman?' 'A Welshman who couldn't swim!' He'd been going to Ireland for years, and one time he was going to visit this pub where he'd made many friends, but they didn't know he was coming. He opened the door, walked in, and there was this guy sitting in the far corner of the pub who saw Grav arrive. He shouted over the pub, 'Aia Ray!' and the whole pub had a tremendous fright, with some running out of the nearest doors, others falling to the floor and crawling under tables, because what they heard was 'IRA'!

I thought the world of him, and loved being in his company. He was great to be with socially. But, he could, from time to time, get on your nerves, and you had to tell him. When broadcasting on S4C there are commercial breaks. So there is a natural break at half time during rugby games. We would go to the adverts, fill in whatever time we had to fill, go to another commercial break and then on to the second half. Well, sometimes, when the first half finished, Grav would grab someone for an interview and then we would go to a break. Then, during the commercial break, we would receive instructions through our earpieces about what we would cover in discussions with our expert guests. So I had to listen to the director through my earpiece saying, 'Right Gar, here's the order of things. Start by talking about this and that, then go on to this. We're going to show try a, b and c,' and so on and so on. But what I would also hear in my earpiece would be Grav's blinking walkie-talkie, 'Hey Sion, Sion, how was that? Was that OK?' for about two minutes, and we only had three minutes of adverts! I came close to shouting, 'Shut up, I want to know what's happening next!' But he needed that reassurance, didn't he? So we came up with the phrase, 'Grav, Grav, radio silence, radio silence.' Of course, it was a mixture of his nervousness and his enthusiasm, and he so wanted to please. He was a huge and legendary character.

Frank Hennessy

Ray and I travelled together a lot during our long-running series, *On The Road*. Ray would often join me at some point along the way to our destination – say Builth Wells, heading for Bangor or some other town in the far north. He would park up, transfer his stuff into my car, and usually ask if I was OK to drive the first 60 miles, and then he'd take over. Really? Ray would inevitably fall asleep immediately, only to wake up as we arrived at the appointed spot three hours later – fully refreshed and raring to go. I felt a bit like a lonely chauffeur.

On one trip, heading for Holyhead, I decided to keep him awake by engaging him in a riveting conversation on a subject that was close to his heart. So I fed him the question – 'Who is the greatest Welsh rugby player of all time?'

'Whoof! That's a good one,' said Ray, staring out as the countryside flashed by, obviously deep in concentration.

I waited in vain for his answer. It soon became apparent that he was in fact in a deep sleep. Almost four hours later, as we arrived at the hotel, his eyes opened and, without a pause, he shouted 'Barry John!'

I was amazed he'd even remembered my question, let alone formulated an answer!

'Barry John,' says I. 'The greatest of all time. Are you sure?'

'Absolutely,' replied Ray. 'He was the king.'

'What about Gareth?' I probed.

'Oh, yeah,' says Grav. 'Gareth was the greatest.'

'And what about Gerald, JPR, Delme, Phil Bennett?' I followed up.

'Them too,' he replied.

I was confused. 'Come on Ray, they can't all be the greatest.'

'But they were, Frankie – all the greatest.'

'What about you then? Where did you rate among the best?' I wondered.

'Oh,' he said, 'I was just lucky to be in one of the greatest teams ever assembled. They made me look good.'

It was an insight into the humility of the man. And I loved him for it.

*

One night we were sharing a room in Barmouth when I began to feel unwell. After dinner I made my excuses and went up to our room early, leaving the team to have their usual convivial hour or two in the bar before retiring. I had a pain across my shoulders which I thought was some kind of muscle strain. It gradually got worse and no amount of painkillers seemed to do any good. It turned out I was having a severe angina attack which would return a few weeks later as a full-blown heart attack.

Grav and I were both heavy smokers at the time, and I lit up a fag and lay on my bed trying to find a comfortable position, blowing smoke into the air. The cigarette did nothing to ease my discomfort. In fact, it seemed to make it worse. Stubbing it out, I threw a pillow and a few blankets onto the floor, hoping a firm base might help. It did not, and I lay there tossing and turning. A couple of hours later the bedroom door burst open and in staggered Grav.

'Frankie, where are you?' he called, staring at the empty bed.

'I'm down here on the floor, Ray,' I replied.

'What's happened? Are you ill? Do you want a drink? Fancy a ciggy?'

'No thanks mate,' I squeaked through gritted teeth. 'In fact I don't think I'll ever smoke again.'

'Crikey!' exclaimed Ray. 'Are you sure?'

'Absolutely,' says I.

Ray's eyes lit up. 'Can I have your fags then?'

I was helpless with laughter and doubled up in pain at the same time.

Only Grav could do that.

The following day's show went well, apart from an attack of killer seagulls. For some reason Ray seemed to have an irrational fear of birds – especially big ones. During a live broadcast from Cardiff Castle, Grav was interviewing the head gardener when a magnificent peacock came up behind him and gave an ear-splitting cry. It must have seen Ray as a competitor, and as he turned to see what had made such a terrible screech, the bird went into full display mode with its beautiful tail feathers fanned out into a most impressive sight. Ray almost fainted before the gardener explained, 'Ray, this is one of our prized feathered residents, the dominant peacock. He's just warning you off, stay calm.'

'A peacock!' exclaimed Ray. 'What fabulous colours! I've never seen anything like it. But what's that brown dull-looking one with him?'

'Ah, that's the female,' replied the groundsman. 'It's a peahen.'

Grav was in raptures. 'Peacock, peahen, I love it.' Then,

seeing a dozen much smaller birds following on, 'Ah look, they've got their babies with them.'

'No, Ray,' said the gardener. 'Those are pigeons.'

Priceless!

*

While having dinner at a very nice restaurant in Criccieth, Ray spotted a very distinguished-looking man at the next table, who was in the company of three other well-dressed diners. Without a word to me, Grav got up and, tapping the chap on the shoulder, said, 'Excuse me, but are you an actor?'

The stranger, obviously unsettled at this intrusion, said, 'An actor? Certainly not!'

'Are you sure?' persisted Ray.

'Absolutely,' came the reply.

'A conductor then,' continued our boy. 'The Hallé, or the Royal Philharmonic perhaps.'

The poor man was getting het up by now.

'Look! I have nothing to do with the theatre or music. You are very mistaken. Now, please can I get on with my meal?'

'Sorry,' says Ray, 'So what are you then?'

'Well, if you must know, I am a consultant psychiatrist.'

'Ah,' says Grav triumphantly, 'I knew you were in show business.'

We finished the meal in silence, apart from Ray shouting 'Cockadoodledooo' as we left.

Roy Noble

I first met Grav in the media world. I had seen him play rugby for Llanelli, the Scarlets, and also for Wales over the years, but it was in the media world that I first met him, and we became huge friends. The first thing I noticed was that he didn't have any self-confidence, and there was an air of insecurity around him most of the time. He would arrive in the mornings for example to broadcast, and the first thing he would ask would be, 'How's my voice? How's my voice? Is it OK? Do you think they could listen to my voice today?'

I remember going with him to broadcast from Dublin. We had a programme to present, and we were staying overnight. We'd been out, you know, on the 'sherbets' the night before, and arrived back at the hotel about 3.30am. The phone in my room started ringing, and I picked it up and said,

'Uh, hello?'

'Roy? Grav here.'

'What do you want?'

'Tell me Roy, tell me. What do you really think of me really?'

At 3.30 in the morning!

The next morning we went down to pay. Everything was paid for except the phone calls. I had phoned my wife of course, and my mother who wasn't well at the time. They had Punts in Ireland then, not Euros, so I had a Punt to pay. Grav came up to me and asked, 'Can you pay my bill? I haven't got any Punts. You pay and I'll pay you back next week.' He had made 160 Punts worth of calls during the night. He'd phoned everyone in Wales and Ireland that would be prepared to speak to him, to give him a bit of confidence because he was feeling a bit low. You see, he would feel low sometimes before rising again to be on top of the world. What a character.

He would take you as you were, your strengths and weaknesses. I remember once, me now, so passionate about rugby – I had played for Ammanford, not that I was a good player, and Ammanford were bad at the time. The village was a dangerous place to be when the team was short of players. I was picked up once to go on the bus when they were playing away, me on one wing, and the bus driver playing on the other wing in brogues. He didn't have any boots. Anyway, I remember walking into this big room with Grav in Cardiff. There were international rugby players from everywhere there, some from South Africa, from New Zealand, from Australia, France, Scotland. Everybody was there. Ray was in the middle of the room chatting with Bill Beaumont, and he said, 'Roy! Royo come here, come here!' So over I went, and Grav said, 'Right then Roy, this is Bill Beaumont, captain of England, captain of the Barbarians, captain of the Lions. Bill, meet Roy, Ammanford Seconds!' Grav made me feel one of them you see, because I had also played the game.

Going back to that radio broadcast out in Dublin when he phoned me in the middle of the night. For some reason, the producer had arranged for Ray and myself as presenters to share the guests and interview them alternately. He said, 'Roy, you interview the first guest, and then Ray the second,' and so on. It was my turn to interview, and who walked in but Mary O'Hara, the Singing Nun as she was called. Well! Ray had fallen in love with her before she sat down. So, it was me to interview her and ask her all the questions, but Ray was dying to ask her some questions. Very suddenly, before I knew it, I felt him put his hand under the table, and start to squeeze me in a very sensitive place... and I couldn't say a word... and he ended up asking her about six or seven questions on his own!

I remember broadcasting with him from Pwllheli, at

the Butlin's Camp. We had a problem in the room that we were sharing, in that the taps in the bathroom took half an hour to three-quarters of an hour to fill the bath. There was no shower, so we had to use the bath. Ray said, 'We don't have time. We'll have to go in the bath together!' And that's what happened. Both of us in the bath at the same time! He told my son years later, 'Listen, I've had a bath with your father, and I'm telling you now, your father has nothing to be embarrassed about!'

He was on his own. He had a personality that would fill an aircraft hangar! We had an invitation, my wife and I, to his home in Mynydd-y-Garreg. We had a competition, a blind whiskey tasting competition. We had to taste the whiskey without knowing what whiskey it was or where it was from. He had a barrel, which was a present from his mother, which was split in the middle and would open up and was full of whiskey bottles. The test was to try to guess if the whiskey came from Scotland or Ireland or maybe Bourbon from America. Once you had decided on the country, you had to guess what part of that country; for example, in Scotland, did it come from an island, like Islay, or from the Spey Valley or somewhere like that, or from what part of Ireland, the north or the south? By the end of the night the big question was guessing which room we were in! He was on his own, and being in his company was a privilege.

Carolyn Hitt

The flame-haired centre from Mynydd-y-Garreg burned with passion for his country and channelled patriotic fervour into every performance. A shoulder injury that took him out for the entire 1977 Five Nations kept his cap count to 23. But a post-rugby career that encompassed acting and broadcasting ensured his folk hero status kept growing. By the time of his sadly premature death, following complications from diabetes in 2007, he was a national treasure. No-one donned the red jersey with a greater sense of what it is to be Welsh than Grav.

Like so many, I frequently experienced the joy of a Grav pep talk. When first asked to write about rugby, even though I loved the game, I worried that I wasn't qualified to hold an opinion. But each time I bumped into Grav our motivational routine was the same. I would get a hug, he'd tell me how much he had enjoyed that week's piece, and if someone happened to be passing at the same time he would grab them and tell them why they should read my column too. It was such a lovely confidence boost.

I watched him show that same generosity of spirit as he gave a speech before Wales' World Cup game against Australia. The room was filled with corporate movers and shakers but there was also a family who had won competition tickets to the match. And Grav ensured that their youngest member – a 13-year-old Scarlets fan – was treated like the star guest. Throughout his talk he kept throwing lines in the

boy's direction, addressing him by name as the youngster beamed with pride.

He was such a magical communicator. Who can forget those tactile touchline interviews, those last-minute pats on players' backs as they ran out of the tunnel, and those hilarious turns of phrase as Gavin Henson was told he was 'cool for cats' or Scottish coach Matt Williams was greeted with 'Here he is – Robert Redford!' His irrepressible broadcasting style was an antidote to the cynical side of professional sport.

Grav was a tonic in human form. He always made you

feel better – whether it was with a generous compliment, an enthusiastic chat or just a huge bear hug. It now seems especially poignant that Wales got the chance to tell Grav just how much he was loved. Completely without ego, he never seemed to realise just how special he was. He was always too busy telling other people why they should feel good about themselves.

I still can't believe Grav has gone. All that energy and humour, passion and patriotism, his tenderness and courage, his sheer zest for life. How can all that just cease so cruelly? The toughest centre with the softest heart, a doting dad and affectionate friend, he was unique.

All of Wales feels his loss but, of course, our grief cannot compare with that of Mari and his daughters Manon and Gwenan. I'll never forget talking to Grav about his girls while on the Lions tour of Australia. His eyes filled with tears as he explained how much he was missing them. He was the ultimate family man.

Sulwyn Thomas

Radio Cymru were broadcasting nationally and locally simultaneously at one point. Jonsi nationally, and Raymond Gravell entertaining the audiences of Swansea and the western valleys. Well, one day he was in Mynydd-y-Garreg in my friend Mansel Thomas' house, broadcasting in the midst of a Macmillan Coffee Morning.

That morning Grav was on his own. To me, as one who

was used to working with complicated technical machines with a sound engineer sitting next to me, the thought of Grav having to cope on his own amazed me. Mansel was worried, and he asked me to pop over. On the way from Carmarthen to Mansel's home it was Jonsi on the car radio as I reached the house. Ironically, the people of Mynydd-y-Garreg were not going to be able to listen to their hero that morning.

Anyway, I met Grav, struggling and panicking in the hallway by the house phone. The challenge when broadcasting live was to get a connection with Cardiff. Quite simple you might think. He had a box in his hand and a mike, and all that was needed was to use the phone landline to link with the studio in Cardiff. But it all turned into a pantomime. Keith 'Bach' Davies, his producer, phoned dozens of times and the minutes were running out before it was time to broadcast.

It was quite obvious that Gravell was not technical in any way or form! But, somehow, the right buttons were pressed. And it was amazing to see and hear Grav doing his stuff as if he hadn't a care in the world about the potential disaster just minutes earlier. A completely natural broadcaster, with everybody ready to help him in any way.

Proper broadcasting practices and procedures didn't worry Grav at all; like interrupting a live broadcast for example – something that was frowned upon as completely irresponsible in those early days. There is a story about him rushing into a studio in Cardiff as Owen Money was broadcasting live on Radio Wales. His line to Owen when he realised his mistake was immortal, 'Sorry Owen, right studio, wrong day.'

Only Grav could do something like that without being seriously told off. Only Grav could hand over the broadcasting reins to the king of Radio Wales broadcasters, Vincent Kane, with the words, 'Now over to you, Vincey baby.' Immortal!

There are so many examples of him worrying about his performances. He would ask over and over if it was acceptable or not. It was the same during his playing days for Llanelli, Wales and the Lions. In the end the coaches had to tell him straight, 'If you are playing poorly, we'll tell you, don't worry. Now go away!' In a matter of minutes he would be back asking the same questions. But you couldn't be angry with him.

But I had to be quite stern with him once. A friend of mine was reopening his garage and was launching a new car on the same evening. I suggested that Grav would be just the man to do the job. He had just stopped playing rugby and was venturing into the broadcasting world. The night was to start at seven o'clock, but there was no sign of the celebrity guest. Half past, eight o'clock, half past eight and the main man had not arrived. I was begged to do the duties, with specific instructions not to mention Grav if he happened to arrive in the middle of ceremonies. And that's exactly what he did, and of course he was ignored.

At the end of the night I had to say something to him. So I started going on about the fact that it was completely unacceptable for him to turn up late to events, and expect the kind of welcome he'd been used to at rugby clubs. He was now a professional and it was so important to be disciplined to protect the good name of the BBC, etc. If this was to happen again, he would not be appointed by broadcasters. And that hit home. The last thing Grav wanted was a closed door to any studio; he loved being in front of a mike. Punctuality was important to him after that.

Yes, broadcasting meant so much to him. There came an order from Cardiff that nobody was allowed to smoke at the BBC studios after a specific date. When I told Grav he wasn't at all happy. He had to have a smoke to calm his nerves and so on. The only conclusion to this, I told him, was that he could no longer broadcast. When the said date arrived, Grav announced that he had given up smoking!

Grav was a soul, a broadcaster and an actor that didn't fully realise that he had so much talent with regard to timing, and the mystical ability to grab his audience. He was aware that he was no ordinary rugby player. He also realised that his fame as a rugby player had given him confidence. But as a performer, he would convey himself as the innocent child. And that was the secret of his appeal beyond the rugby field.

I'll never forget the night when he was the guest speaker at our Clwb Cinio Caerfyrddin (Carmarthen Culinary Club). He was a bundle of nerves and gave the impression that he hadn't prepared a thing. He was only on his feet for 20 minutes, and he didn't say a word about rugby. He just talked about family. After he sat down, the floor was opened for questions. Now, with anyone else, I don't think the audience would have entertained asking a question after such a short speech. But it was Grav who was in front of us, hero and giant. The questions flowed for over an hour, so much was the interest in him. I didn't say much to him at the time, but I'm sure he knew that there would be loads of questions and that he would be so comfortable answering them.

A long time before he fell ill, I went to see him and asked if he could choose four songs for Radio Glangwili (Glangwili Hospital Radio) in Carmarthen. As one who thought the world of the doctors and nurses at the hospital and all the treatments he'd received over the years as a rugby player, he was more than ready to chat about his favourite singers. As you can imagine, Dafydd Iwan was one, Pavarotti another.

He was home that day, looking after his two daughters, Manon and Gwenan. He adored them. Now and again, he would shout at them to be quiet so as not to disturb the recording. Another lovely pantomime – especially when one of the girls was mimicking their father by talking into a plastic toy mike. Grav idolised them and could completely identify with their innocence.

Geraint Lloyd

Oh, memories of Grav! I remember one year there was a gang of us Radio Cymru presenters working from the Royal Welsh Show in Builth Wells, and Grav was with us this particular year. We were all staying together at a hotel in Llandrindod, with many others from the BBC and S4C of course. And you see, Grav was getting up at 5am every morning and would then go for a shower, and that's where he would be, singing or blasting out 'Calon Lân' and 'Sosban Fach' as loud as he could, and waking everybody up! Usually, there was no need to get up early, because breakfast was at around 8.30 to 9am before we all went over to the Show. But no... And it wasn't just the BBC crew that he would wake up, he would wake everybody up in the hotel! But of course, by the time we all got up he would have gotten to know all the staff in the kitchen, and there he'd be helping them as if he'd been working there for years. That's the kind of character he was, he would fill the room with his presence, and everybody would be drawn to him and we had a wonderful week.

One night, I remember we went out for a meal – to a Chinese restaurant I think it was – and we weren't there for ten minutes before Grav started to sing! Everybody would want to speak with him and sit with him, and we had an amazing time. He was like a magnet to people. Very fond memories.

Mal Pope

Stories about Ray Gravell, the ones that I actually can tell!

Ray and I got quite friendly during the years of working together at the BBC in Swansea. At the time, Radio Cymru had moved a couple of programmes to Swansea, as had Radio Wales. So I was broadcasting in English and Ray was broadcasting regularly 'yn Gymraeg'. I remember somebody walking into the main office one afternoon and asking, 'Is Ray Gravell in?' And I went, 'Ahh, can you hear anything?' and they looked around and said, 'No, can't hear anything.' I said, 'In that case, he's not here!'

Because when Ray was anywhere in the building, you would know that he was there, because he was so loud! I kept on thinking to myself that I lived in black and white, whereas Ray Gravell used to live in full technicolour! He was always so generous of spirit every time he would meet me; he'd introduce me to everybody saying, 'Oh, Maldwyn, Maldwyn Pope. Oh, West is best, West is best, West is best!'

He was, amazingly, able to say to people some things which would have got the rest of us arrested! I remember him making some comments to the Editor of Radio Wales at the time, Gaynor Vaughan-Jones, about her appearance. Most of us would have had a slap across the cheek! But no, it was Ray and he got away with anything.

I suppose that one of the stories that really sticks in my mind comes from after he passed away. I got quite friendly with a guy called Merrill Osmond, the lead singer of The Osmonds. He was over in Wales, and we'd done some writing and recording together, and as I was doing the Sunday afternoon programme he came in to be a guest on the show. It was the weekend after Ray had passed away, and in the foyer of the BBC in Llandaff there was a book of condolence. Merrill had seen the service at Stradey Park, and he was just so moved by the effect of Ray's passing on the whole country. And he signed the book of condolence on behalf of the whole Osmond family – who believe they're Welsh, by the way – and I remember him turning to me and saying, 'When my time comes, I hope that I have the same impact on people as Ray obviously had on the people of Wales.' And I thought that was quite an accolade from someone who's had so much adulation during his life. He wanted to have made a mark, just as Ray Gravell did on the people of Wales.

Aneirin Karadog

My memory of Grav, first of all, is growing up with him. His presence would penetrate into our home over the airwaves through his presenting during rugby matches, interviewing players, and commenting with Huw Llywelyn Davies. Their voices were part of our cultural furniture, just like poets and music and stuff like Hogia'r Wyddfa grow into being part of our cultural furniture. Grav's contribution was the same.

I was brought up in Pontardawe in the '80s and moved to Pontypridd in 1990. I supported the Scarlets. Our father had turned us against the Jacks by saying, 'You can't support the Jacks!' When we arrived in Pontypridd I would go down to Sardis Road to see the Scarlets playing and I would also go and see Pontypridd. I supported them as my second team. I would have to hide my Scarlets' shirt under my coat from the people that would know me in Pontypridd. So there was that sort of connection, and through Grav's favourite club too.

Then, fortunately, I got a job with Tinopolis in 2005 and moved out west to live. My introduction to Tinopolis coincided with my first introduction to Grav himself. The reason being that his best friend from his school days at Carmarthen Grammar School for Boys, 'Pinky' Adrian Howells, was our producer on *Wedi 7* and *Heno*. Grav would often have lunch with Adrian at the 'Savoy' in Llanelli, not the healthiest of lunches, mostly sausage and chips, or fish and chips or something like that. Grav would come through the Tinopolis building like a tornado, as he would shout hello to everyone. He had heard that I had started working there, and he knew about me because I had just won the Urdd National Eisteddfod Chair in 2005, the same year as I started there. Grav loved shouting things like 'Karactacus! Karactacus!' in that unforgettable voice of his when he saw me, playing on Latinising Karadog. And that was my first introduction to the head of Tinopolis, Ron Jones, through Grav, in that huge open-plan office. It was quite a surreal moment in a way, as he referred to me by saying, 'Ron, Ron, the poet man. You haven't met the poet yet, have you?' And

Ron answering, 'Don't encourage him. I've heard that he's bad enough as it is!'

Then Grav became part of our daily lives in the area because he was presenting his radio programme in west Wales. Radio Cymru would split at Port Talbot, so, if you lived in the west, Grav would be with you every morning. After listening to his programme I would arrive at work, and the programme would continue in a way because Ray would be phoning Adrian all morning. Adrian would look at his phone and say something like, 'O yffach, I've got work to do here!' and he would complain to us, 'He's phoning me again!' He would phone to discuss betting, rugby, if they were going out for lunch, discussing all kind of things. Grav's personality would penetrate everywhere; his nervousness, his energy and his inability to stay still in any one place for long.

One morning I was invited by Tomos Morse and Keith Davies (Keith Bach), who produced Grav's programme *Grav o'r Gorllewin* (Grav from the West), to write an 'englyn' (poem) for him. They hadn't told him I was coming on his programme. I remember them phoning me, and putting me directly live on air with Grav to talk about the fact that I had recently moved to the west, started working at Tinopolis, and had written an englyn for him. After I read the englyn to him he was apparently in tears. However, if you read a list of your favourite food to him he would probably cry, wouldn't he?! He was such an emotional man.

Grav

Gweld y gorwel wna'r gwladgarwr, gweld cais
See the horizon does the patriot, see the try
    A gweld coch yr heriwr,
    And see the red of the challenger,
Gweld chwedl y genedl wna'r gŵr,
See the legend of the nation does the man,
Un o'r werin yw'r arwr.
One of the folk is the hero.

He appreciated things like that, and then said that he enjoyed listening to the band I was in, Genod Droog, on the radio. He would enjoy a bit of rap and would give encouragement through his wonderful and enticing enthusiasm. In a way, I feel privileged to have met him. I'm aware that he knew so many people: close family, best friends, rugby players, having toured with the Lions. He also collaborated on TV productions, and people shared very poignant moments with him also. But, somehow, he touched everyone in the same way I think.

Hearing then that we had lost him... I received a phone call or text from Adrian Howells that night after hearing of his death, and of course there was a special programme being prepared for *Wedi 7* the next day as a tribute. That was such a difficult experience for so many of us in the studio. The funeral was something very special. I never saw such a thing. Seeing Rhodri Morgan, our First Minister, Dafydd Iwan and Gwyneth Glyn paying tributes to him in different ways. It was a state funeral, and it was a privilege to be present there on that November morning.

I have many warm memories of Grav, and those memories have inspired me to try and spread some of his enthusiasm, especially his enthusiasm for the Welsh language. I did a project recently with children at Ysgol Bro Myrddin, and I took them to Parc y Scarlets and asked them, 'Do you know this man, the man who has a statue outside the stadium?' None of them had any idea of who the statue was, namely Ray Gravell. It shows you how quickly things can disappear, how short the memory is for someone – even a person as remarkable as Grav can become forgotten. It's a truly frightening reality.

One thing I will say is that we have lovely neighbours here in Pontyberem, a couple called Tony and Eirlys. Tony worked with Grav as an engineer years ago. Grav would call him 'cochyn' (ginger) and Tony, a man of Llanelli, had very limited Welsh. But through Grav he learned Welsh, because Grav refused to speak English with him. So that example is there for us to follow. I can speak Welsh with Tony now on a daily basis because Grav had insisted on speaking Welsh with him and that is amazing. Grav was a wonderful example to us all, and his important message is that we strengthen and spread the language by being completely firm.

And lastly, I'd like to add that it was a huge honour for me when the family and Keith Bach contacted me to say that a bust was being made of Grav by John Meirion Morris from Llanuwchllyn. It's a wonderful bust, by the way. They wanted a line to be added to the bust, and they chose the last line of my englyn that I read to him on his radio programme, *Un o'r werin yw'r arwr* (One of the folk is the hero). They felt that the line reflected him as a person, and the line is there on his bust in the BBC foyer in Cardiff. He was one of the folk, wasn't he? And Manon, his daughter, also has the line on her Twitter account, and I feel it a huge honour. As a poet, what more could you want than to have people appreciate your words in such a way.

Also from Y Lolfa:

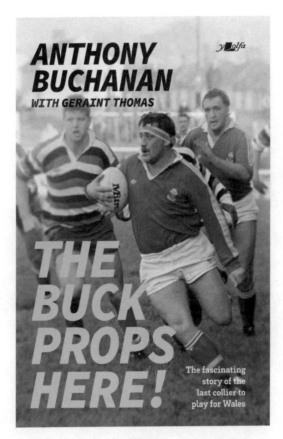

£9.99

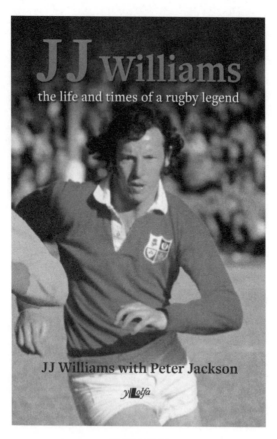

JJ Williams

the life and times of a rugby legend

JJ Williams with Peter Jackson

Y Lolfa

£14.99 (hb)

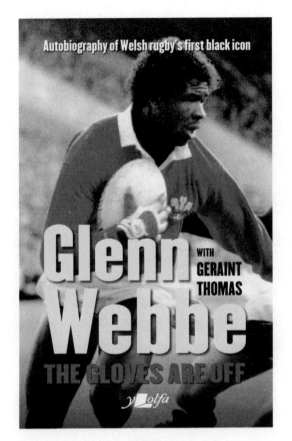

Autobiography of Welsh rugby's first black icon

Glenn Webbe

WITH GERAINT THOMAS

Webbe

THE GLOVES ARE OFF

y Lolfa

£9.99

THE
SENSATIONAL
RUGBY
AUTOBIOGRAPHY

LEE
**THE BYRNE
IDENTITY**
BYRNE

£9.99

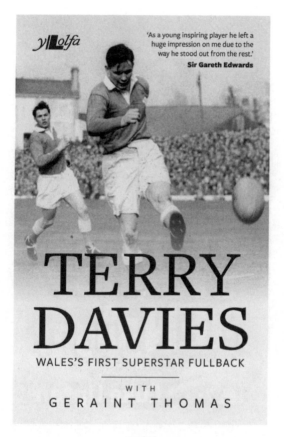

'As a young inspiring player he left a huge impression on me due to the way he stood out from the rest.'

Sir Gareth Edwards

TERRY DAVIES

WALES'S FIRST SUPERSTAR FULLBACK

WITH

GERAINT THOMAS

£9.99

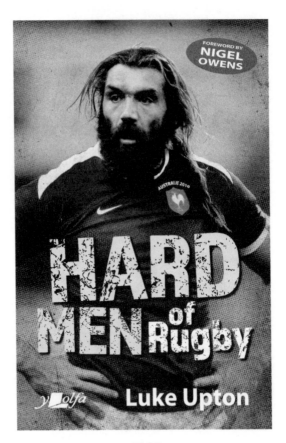

FOREWORD BY
NIGEL
OWENS

HARD
MEN of
Rugby

y Lolfa   Luke Upton

£9.99

LYNN DAVIES

hard men
of WELSH
RUGBY

y Lolfa

£7.95